# CLIPPED
## *INSIDE SOHO'S CLIP JOINTS*

By Maxine White & Michael Lutwyche

# VHC PUBLISHING

*MADE IN BIRMINGHAM, ENGLAND*
*City of a thousand trades*

*This book was written for my children Molly, Billy and Amber.
Also in memory of my father, who sadly passed away some years ago but who is always loved and remembered and was always my best friend.*

Published in Birmingham, England in 2009 by VHC Publishing

ISBN: 978-0-9561302-1-1

All rights reserved.

This book is sold on the condition that it shall not, by way of trade or otherwise, be lent, re-sold, hired out or otherwise circulated without the publisher's written consent in any form of cover or binding other than that in which it is published and without a similar condition being imposed on the subsequent purchaser.

No part of this book may be reproduced or transmitted in any form or by any means, electronic or mechanical including photo-copying, recording or by any information storage and retrieval system, without permission from the publisher in writing

VHC PUBLISHING, PO BOX 14913, BIRMINGHAM, B32 9DU

# Acknowledgements

A huge thank you to Michael, for his hard work, patience (and full stops!) and for being there for me, as a friend, as well as a co-author. Thank you to Mr Fowler for supporting the project, without you this would not have been possible.
Thank you to my two 'special ladies' Ella and Elaine, who have worked so very hard to make this book the best.
'Nebby', thank you for your support and refreshing my mind on things that were not totally clear after all these years, also thank you for those years xx
Thanks to Aunty Shell and JC for being there for me when I was getting stressed you were always on the end of a phone
Thanks to the Sue Fell School of Kickboxing in Burton on Trent and to Kirsty for keeping me focused at all times.
To Jamma and Jo, Snake and Leanne, 'M' (my surrogate mum in Soho), D and I for looking after me while I was in Soho and the rest of the gang, Terry, my best friend for dragging me away from everything to the football when I found things difficult, thanks to you all xx
Thanks Jo my personal hairdresser and Dean for being themselves and not letting me get above myself.
And last of all and most importantly, to Steve, my mum and my amazing children, I love you all dearly. Thanks for putting up with me whilst writing this book, as some things I thought I had put away for ever xx

*Maxine*

Thanks to Maxine and Steve. Without Maxine this book would not have existed. Steve with his wise counsel, made sure that we both kept things into perspective.
Thanks to my good friend Mark for his advice on all aspects of this book.
Thanks to Steve Fowler for believing in me and this project.
Thanks to Carl for the advice, time and most importantly the inspiration.
Thanks to Ian and Simon from Excel Printing for technical support, guidance and as always a 1st class job.
Thanks to the literary and proof-reading team Elaine & Ella, of NDC H/C. This book wouldn't be what it is without your input. I was very fortunate to have your friendship, expertise and advice to call upon. My debt to you is immeasurable and it will never be forgotten.
Thanks to Kenichi, my friend from Japan, for his time and effort in translating the Japanese version of synopsis. Thanks to 'Hippy Pat' Murphy and Matty Pedley.
Thanks to Dandy and Erica, Jonesy and Karen, Steamy and Mel and Bob Busby, for their support and friendship, as always, which is never taken for granted and always appreciated.
There are two types of friend in this world. The one sort disappear when you encounter life's problems, the other kind come running towards you. I am truly fortunate to have a handful of the latter.

My work on this book is dedicated to the memory of Mark Donovan 'Blue' Thomas
Rest in peace my old friend, you will never be forgotten. Till we meet again…

*Michael Lutwyche*

# CLIPPED
## INSIDE SOHO'S CLIP JOINTS

| | |
|---|---|
| INTRODUCTION | Page 7 |
| ROAD TO HELL | Page 11 |
| HIT AND RUN | Page 21 |
| RUNAWAY | Page 25 |
| SOHO | Page 39 |
| THE SWITCH | Page 43 |
| THE QUEEN'S HIGHWAY | Page 61 |
| HALLUCINATION | Page 85 |
| CHASING THE DRAGON | Page 89 |
| YOUR MISSUS IS A NUTTER | Page 97 |
| PEEP SHOW | Page 105 |
| GOING DUTCH | Page 113 |
| HAFT NA FLOOSE | Page 127 |
| SOHO PEOPLE | Page 131 |
| WHEN WE LAUGH AT THE FIELDS OF REGRET | Page 143 |

# Introduction

## Clip joint

Origin: 1930–35, Americanism

Slang.
A business, esp. a place of entertainment that makes a practice of overcharging or cheating customers.

A clip joint or fleshpot is a strip club or entertainment bar, offering adult entertainment, in which customers are routinely fleeced; paying excessive amounts of money for poor, or no, goods or services in return.

Typically, a clip joint entices business with the underlying suggestion of freely available sex. On the premise of this invariably nebulous promise, they charge excessively high prices for watered-down drinks, and then eject customers when they become unwilling or unable to spend more money. Due to the illicit nature of the services on offer, the customer (victim) will be reluctant to contact the police or take any recourse through official or legal channels.

A typical scam is when a customer is shown in and offered a drink or the company of a hostess at their table. Acceptance means they will be presented with an outrageously inflated bill, sometimes for several hundred pounds, for the drink, service charges, or hostess's company.
Immediate payment is demanded on pain of criminal charges or the threat of physical violence. Clip joints exist on the fringes of legality as there is no law against overcharging and the onus is on any customer to discover what, and how much they are paying in advance of any purchase they may make.

However, some clip joints tout for business near legitimate clubs, enticing passing pedestrians in by surreptitiously presenting themselves as the representatives of the legitimate club, thus lulling their intended victim into a false sense of security.
Clip joint customers find a ticket counter at street level where they pay admission before going down to the bar below. There they are offered usually watered down and overpriced drinks with no tariff openly displayed and the uninvited company of a hostess at their table who will inevitably order the most expensive drinks, usually 'cocktails'.

The unwary victim will then be presented with an inflated bill. Protests or non-payment results in accusations of theft of services with the threat of police action or physical harm unless payment is made.

## Soho

In amongst the bright lights of the up-market leisurely heart of London's licit entertainment oasis, the West End, with its shops, restaurants, cinemas, and theatres, lies the shady square mile of bustling, if diminishing sex trade which is Soho.

Soho is named after a hunting cry, dating back to the time when Soho was a small village on the outskirts of London surrounded by fields

By the mid 19th century Soho was home and host to a transient and impoverished population of the poor, the itinerant and the immigrant. A number of public houses, music halls and theatres blossomed and it soon became largely identified as a cosmopolitan entertainment area.
Music Halls in particular flourished. By 1866 there were 33 listed as open in the city. These reputable, if bawdy, places of entertainment attracted pickpockets, thieves and prostitutes who best plied their trade in crowded places.
By the turn of the century, cheap accommodation abounded in Soho and attracted a throng of bohemian but impoverished writers, poets and painters who settled in the area taking advantage of the affordable but exotic eating houses established by immigrants catering to the influx of disaffected, poverty stricken intellectuals. This socio-economic structure continued and developed up until WW2.

Post WW2 Soho became synonymous with organised crime, drugs and the sex industry and the emerging music scene of Jazz and Skiffle. The area's anti-authoritarian counter culture flourished. Prostitutes were commonplace on virtually every street corner of Soho's square mile.

In 1959 the government introduced the 'Street Offences Act' which drove prostitution off the streets. The act made it illegal for:

'A common prostitute to loiter or solicit in a public place for the purpose of prostitution.'

And it also decreed that:

'A constable may arrest without warrant anyone he finds in a street or public place and suspects, with reasonable cause, to be committing an offence under this section.'

With lucrative, relatively easy money to be made the sex trade simply moved off the streets and into the warren of flats and businesses of Soho.

Strip clubs appeared, many of which were merely fronts for prostitution. Signs, which can still be seen today, advertising things like 'models' or 'foreign student', appeared at the communal entrances to many flats. It wasn't hard for visitors to the area to realise what 'services' these women were offering. By the early 60s Soho was, it is estimated, host to over a hundred strip-clubs. In 1960 a sex cinema called the Compton Cinema Club opened in Old Compton Street. The first clip joints also appeared during the 60s, solely with the intention of ripping off tourists new to 'Swinging London' with the promise of a good time.

In the 70s the area saw the proliferation of sex shops which sold erotica, sex toys and pornography. In Soho there was an estimated 59 of these establishments. Some of these shops also offered an under the counter or backroom services and sold illegal pornography. This black economy was able to flourish due to the complicity of the police at that time, a partnership that culminated in the launch of 'Operation Countryman', an investigation into corruption across the Metropolitan Police. The investigation was initially aimed at the City of London Police, but it was soon extended to cover the Metropolitan Police. It was centred on the Vice Squad and accusations that criminals were bribing officers to turn a blind eye to certain crimes. After six years and at a cost of £4million it emerged that over 400 police officers had lost their jobs as a result of Operation Countryman. The investigation recommended that 300 police officers should face criminal proceedings over bribery allegations; to date no officer has ever been charged as a result of the findings of Operation Countryman.

# Road to Hell

I often wonder if it was being the only child of hard working parents who sent me to a nursery from babyhood, which made me yearn for friendships and to find excitement outside of my home .and if it was the steadfast, loving stability I had there that gave me the courage to leave

As a kid I was quite a tomboy and I used to play mostly with boys, especially Peter and John. They lived next door the bungalow my parents had built in Uttoxeter. I always looked after John my 'little brother' who was five years younger than me. We were instant best friends and soon inseparable and still are now.

His brother Peter was always the sensible one. He would have done well in Soho. When we were kids and queued at the ice cream van he would wait till the very last; trying to get one of the other kids to buy him an ice cream.

After school we would rush out onto the local green to play football.
We would build dens, climb trees and make bows and arrows.
I can't remember having any female friends at that time.
Being the eldest I always got the blame for everything, from balls through windows to stealing fruit out of gardens.

Just down the road a family of gypsies (or 'tinkers' as my father called them) moved in to a huge bungalow they had built. They had a lad called Len who became part of our gang. Regardless of the weather, Len always wore Wellington boots and shorts.

He was, I think, my first love. Len was just so different to anyone else. Even at six, he drove cars round his dad's land without a care in the world and was quite wild.

I liked his wildness, it was exciting. On occasion, the council would close the bypass and he would race horses bareback up and down the road.

His family were best friends with the famous bare-knuckle fighter Bartley Gorman.
One or two of the neighbours would comment to my mother that it wasn't wise to let me mix with a gypsy. But, his manners to my parents were perfect. So, she would laugh and say that he was better mannered than half the kids round there.
Even now, I see Len on occasion, he still lives nearby

My father was always very protective of me, but I think he enjoyed seeing me as a tomboy and would often come out to watch us play football.
A Nottingham Forest fan, he went in goal sometimes, giving us all grief if we didn't put one past him. He took me to the football most weekends and to away games travelling all over the country.

We always stood on the Trent End of the ground, taking a fizzy pop crate for me to stand on. Then it was a sit down fish and chips meal with mushy peas and mint sauce. After that we went to the old ice stadium to watch Nottingham Panthers ice-hockey team. For the last hour me and my father would get our skates on and take to the ice.
I still follow Forest, going to a few games a season.

I remember a weekend when my father had been invited to The Royal Albert Hall for a Royal Navy Function.
Suddenly we were on our way to London.
I was really excited; I hadn't been to London before.
After we watched the parade, my father stayed on at the function, catching up with old comrades.

Mother and I went shopping in Kensington.

It fascinated me, the busy place, the weird dress of the people and the amazing clothes shops.
It was all so different to Uttoxeter.

The street lights seemed brighter; the whole place was so alive and buzzing. There were punk rockers walking round with crazy hair in different colours, pillar box red, bright greens and blue. I thought their clothing was great. They wore tartan trousers with straps on them. The girls wore black fishnets and Doc Marten boots. There was music blasting out from some of the shops.

The place was fascinating.

I knew then that one day, when I was old enough, I would go back to London


When I was about ten, my grandparents became ill and we travelled to Bingham in Nottingham, where they lived, most days and most weekends to look after them. I did voluntary work after school for an hour most nights helping out in the nursing home where my gran was, giving out the drinks.
I enjoyed that.

While my mother and father were looking after my Grandparents, I hung out at the local shop with some local kids. They were a bit of a bad crowd and introduced me to lighter fuel and glue sniffing. I wanted to fit in so I tried both. The first time I was sick everywhere.

I didn't know where I was. I didn't enjoy that so I didn't bother again.

One day, some of the kids went to the park to sniff glue. One lad inhaled loads and became really ill. I was so scared that I ran home and told my father. He came to help straight away but by the time my dad got to the boy he was in a really bad way.

My father sent one of the older kids back to my granddad's house to phone for an ambulance. The ambulance came quickly but it was too late. The boy died on his way to the hospital. I hadn't even known his name.

It could quite easily have been me.

Around the same time, we used visit a childless Auntie in a nursing home in Skegness. During the visit I found sherry in her room and helped myself, getting quite tipsy on it. Auntie found this amusing, decided that it showed character, and took a shine to me. When she died owning a chain of hairdressing shops, she remembered me in her will and left me a trust fund for my education.
My parents decided on a private education and so they arranged for me to take an entrance exam to Derby High School for Girls.

At the time I thought it would be exciting. I was always reading Enid Blyton books that featured boarding schools and the fun they had.

Oh, how different reality was.

Even though my parents had the money to send me there and my mother and father were comfortably off, they couldn't compete with the likes of the others at the school. I remember my mother struggling to pay for a new school blazer. It had to be purchased from an exclusive shop in Derby

The school was full of snooty girls.

One girl, Nina, laughed at my dad for picking me up in an old Toyota car. Nina's 'pater' owned a number of shops and drove as Mercedes.

Bang!

I punched her and she went down. But her bigger sister gave me a black eye in return.

I lied to my father when he saw the black eye. I told him I had been hit by netball.

I just didn't fit in. It wasn't long before my tomboy ways got the better of me and most days ended in a brawl. After three months the head asked my parents to take me out of the school. My mother was disappointed, but my father, coming from a family of 14 from a rough part of Nottingham, understood.

Friargate House was very different to what you would expect at a private school and I fitted in straight away. I became the best of friends with a girl called Lucy. We were very close, in fact we became inseparable. She was tall and very slim and scared of her own shadow. I was short, stocky and wasn't scared of anyone.

The crowd we knocked about with were into the punk scene. It attracted me with its loud, fast beats. The bands swore and didn't care what people thought.

That was the shock factor I loved.

My mother wanted a girly girl in wear pretty dresses and hair in ribbons, but this wasn't me. I wanted to live in jeans and tracksuit bottoms. However, she employed a seamstress called Miss Mouse. Miss Mouse, on my mother's instructions, made me frilly, flowery dresses. I hated them.

The punk thing suited me.

I liked the images I was seeing on television and in the newspapers.
It symbolised everything my mother didn't want me to be.
I loved it when people would cross the road just because I was looking wild with my green spiked hair, ripped trousers and earrings in my ears, nose and anywhere else I could put an earring.

I loved being the rebel.

One day, I used my dad's shaver and shaved off my long blonde hair on both sides until I had the perfect Mohican.

That was the closest I've ever been to seeing my dad cry.

He was devastated.
But I kept this hair cut for years, despite problems at school with teachers insisting I wore a hat in class. I wasn't the only one. There used to be three of us with hats on.

I started mixing with a crowd of punks a fair bit older than myself. They had all left school. Most days they hung out in the market square in Derby.
It was the thrill of their 'don't care' attitude that attracted me.

I started playing. truant from school and we sat in Derby market place drinking cider and abusing anyone who dared question us; being a pain to all who passed by.
We always met up in The Star pub in the old market place in Uttoxeter.

There, I began drinking at thirteen.

Towards the end of my school years I met a black Tim in the Blue Note bar in Derby. Tim was a bad boy. He was into street fighting and selling weed. Uttoxeter had no more than two black people living there.
Again I was playing the rebel.
But, once the shock value of being with him had waned, we were soon over.

I started a college catering course in Burton on Trent and became friends with a girl called Mary. We would go to a pub across the road from the college called The Dog.

One day, we met a couple of black lads with wet-look gelled curly hair. I quite liked black men and was attracted to one of them. After a while, they asked us to skip college and go round to their place for a drink and to play cards. We trusted them, so skipped college and went with them.

On the way, they were full of beans and humorous, laughing with us as we walked to their house.

Even on good day, Burton was a dreary, grey and dirty place. The breweries scattered around it filled the air with the pungent smell of their fermenting yeast. The house, when we got there, was in Burton's roughest area; the outside of it was dirty and dilapidated. It was no better inside. It looked as if it hadn't been touched for years, with old fashioned curtains and 70s wallpaper. It was dirty everywhere and the musty smell of damp hit me as soon as we entered.

The lads showed us in through the hallway, across ripped worn carpet, and then led us into a filthy kitchen/dining room that had a soiled sofa bed in it.

We heard a click and the front door was locked behind us by man in his late twenties. He was older than the two lads and was one of three other men already in the house.

Then, the danger we were in hit me; hard.

We were two young girls of sixteen in a locked house with five older men.

I was terrified.
We didn't really know these guys.
We had been stupid to just go with them.
No one knew where we were.

Some old style reggae music played in the background and the two lads we arrived with had sat down at a table and got out some cards. This dispelled my fears and I felt better, even a bit silly that I had suspected their motives. After all, there were the cards and we were going to do what they had brought us to the house to do.

Before we were dealt a hand, the mood abruptly changed.
My first instincts had been right,

'Right! Shall we have some fun with these two little ladies?' One of the older men said

My fear returned as panic but it was too late to do anything.

The biggest of the three older men lunged for me and roughly pushed me down onto the sofa bed. The others in the room egged him on. They were almost squealing with delight as he did what he wanted with me. I struggled, shouted and swore but it was no good, he was big and much stronger than me. Once he had finished, the other two older men took turns. I was held down while each had their way with me.

Mary, who had kept quiet throughout my whole ordeal, was shaking with the realisation that she was next. She was raped too but only by one of the older men.
I was treated more violently.
I was, they said, the mouthy one.


After they had finished with us we sat there crying and hugging each other. We begged them to please let us go, but they just laughed; getting off on our distress and pleading.

Rape, and keeping us prisoner gave them power.

Eventually one of them unlocked the front door but we sat there for a few minutes, unsure whether to make a move for the door. Was this all part of their game? If we made a move for the door would they lock it again before we got there and rape us again?

Finally, we got up and made a fearful run for the front door. The filthy hall seemed longer and darker somehow as we ran for our lives.
But, all that followed us from the kitchen was the sound of their laughter.

As we walked back to the town centre, Mary was in pieces and crying uncontrollably.
Not me.
All I felt was emptiness.
No anger, no hatred.
Just pain and guilt.

We went our separate ways.
On the hour long bus journey back to Uttoxeter I was sure everyone was staring at me. I was sure they all knew exactly what had happened to me.

I couldn't face people, so stared fixedly out of the window at the passing fields full of sheep with their innocent new-born lambs, dreading that someone may sit next to me and want a conversation when I sorely needed to be alone.

It rained on me on the way home, grey and miserable; like me.

No-one was home. I ran upstairs and ran a scorching hot bath. I needed to scrub away the filth of the day, scrubbing and scrubbing until my skin was red raw.

Finally I felt clean. Clean, but numb. I still hadn't really cried yet.

My parents got in from work shortly after I got out of the bath. I felt so uneasy with them. I had this overwhelming feeling that they would know, straight away, what had happened to me. I couldn't bear my father to know that his little girl had been repeatedly raped because she had been stupid enough to go to a strange house with strange men.

He would be devastated.
What if he blamed me?
I would just keep quiet.

We had tea and sat down to watch television together but they kept asking me if there was something wrong.

Maybe, I could tell them some other time, when I was older, when it was all in the past. When it didn't matter any more.
But not then, it was too raw. I just couldn't bring myself to say anything. I could tell nobody. It had to be shoved away. One of life's big secrets. A story never to be told.

There was a knock at the front door and my father went to answer it. He spoke to a man and a woman for a couple of minutes. My father came back. A policeman and a policewoman were with him

They looked straight at me, their faces grim.
My father's face seemed to be saying 'What have you done now?'

The police said they wanted to ask me a few questions. I panicked; my insides doing somersaults. They started gently, asking about college and the friends I had there, but I knew what was coming next.

They had been told about the rape.

They were very good with me and convinced me that it wasn't my fault. It was unbearably exhausting having to re-live the rape over and over again and afterwards I felt as if I had run an emotional marathon. They left at last but said they would be back the next day to see if I had remembered anymore details.

Now my parents knew it all and I felt even emptier.

They were devastated and hurt that I hadn't told them, begging me to tell them why I'd said nothing. I couldn't properly explain my deep sense of shame; that I felt it was my own fault, that I didn't want them to be disappointed in me.

The same two police officers returned the next day. They had arrested the three older men, but not the two younger ones that had led us to the house. Two of the rapists were brothers from a notorious Burton family and well known to the police. The third man was their relation.

The police explained in detail what I would have to go through in court and asked: Was I brave enough? Could I face those men again? I nodded.

The empty feeling seemed to be growing inside me. I wanted it all to go away.

My parents told me I was brave, they pampered and cared for me like I was a four year old again. They were determined that their little angel would not be hurt again. Everyone seemed to know what was best for me; smothering me with affection.

I wanted to yell 'let me breathe!'

I knew that this was how it was going to be from now up until the court case.

By the time that day arrived. I was an empty shell, feeling nothing. My mother insisted that I must look smart for court. I wore a blouse and a skirt which I hated with a passion. My father wore a dark blue suit. He looked as empty as I felt.
The journey to court was very subdued; we didn't say a word to each other. There was nothing to say. Everything was irrelevant compared to what had happened and what was about to happen. We drew up to the looming court building, the grey stony walls enveloping us in gloom.

Once inside, we were introduced to the barrister who would be prosecuting the men. Everything was done to put me at ease. My dad took charge. He hadn't been able to protect me from what had happened and he was doing his best to shield me now.

We were shown to a room where we were to wait until it was my turn to give evidence. When it was time, I was led into the court.
I would be lying if I said I could remember everything about the court case.
It's a blur.
I just remember being cold, and wood, everywhere.

What I do remember vividly is the predominantly female family of the rapists hurling abuse at me; shouting things like 'Slag' and 'Slut'. I felt really intimidated by that. One of them swore and shouted that if they ever saw me in Burton they would do me over. Every day of the trial, they harangued me and my parents as we left court.

The court case went on for a number of days; the details are hazy as I think I have, over the years, blocked it out of my mind. At some point during the trial I saw Mary with her parents. We didn't speak; we just looked at each other.

That was the last time I saw her, I can't ever remember seeing her again after that. I'm glad I didn't, as I don't know what we would have talked about.

After a few days, all three men were found guilty and I think they got five years each but I'm not sure. After the verdict, their enraged families were waiting for us outside and we endured a torrent of violent abuse. One of the sisters threatened they would be coming to get us, but they never did.
I stayed away from Burton and didn't go back to the college again, I was ashamed of myself for getting into the situation and letting it all happen. I blamed myself for a long time.

I lived under the ugly shadow of it all for years.

# Hit and Run

I started back at college in Derby, studying catering and hotel management. I made friends with one of the lecturer's daughters. Most dinner times we went to the nearest pub. It wasn't long before I was expelled, for fighting. The drink had played a major part.

Getting drunk was what most of us did back then.
With few qualifications, I ended up working in a local biscuit factory in Uttoxeter. I lost that job as I was never there on time or they could smell drink on me after dinnertime.

During my short time there I met my next boyfriend, Colin. Colin was cute with a mop of dark curly hair and tattooed, rugged looks. After a while, fed up with the same routine, we ran away to Skegness together, drawn there by its appealing youth scene.

Punks, mods and rockers all mixed, and would meet on the sea-front most evenings on scooters and motorbikes. It was good just hanging out with them and finding a little club that played the latest sounds: The Specials, The Beat and Madness.

We had a little bit of money but not much, so as my Auntie's solicitor was also in Skegness, I went to claim the rest of the money now I had finished school. As long as the money paid our rent things went well. It was when it ran out things went wrong.

We tried, but we couldn't get any work. We thought of asking our parents but I had left home on bad terms. I knew that my father would still do anything for me, but couldn't ask him. Colin's parents never had any money. His father was an alcoholic who spent all his on drink.

I don't know why but I suddenly decided I was going to become a prostitute. It seemed quite easy and glamorous work in the movies so it had got to be worth a go, I thought.

After what had happened to me previously at college, I know this was a strange idea. But I wasn't scared of men - I just didn't have any kind of feeling for them.

I know now that what happened in Burton was the driving force that set me on the road to London. All that I did and what I ended up doing, came from that.

There were some nice hotels in Skegness. From what I had read in books and seen on the television, prostitutes sat in the bars of posh hotels and waited to be approached.

I didn't have a clue.

We planned that I was to sit in a bar and wait to be chatted up. Colin would be close by to make sure nothing bad happened.

The first couple of nights, nothing. Nobody spoke to me. Finally, a man approached and offered to buy me a drink. I accepted. He was late 40s, in a business suit and was the short, plump, golfing sort. He looked like he had plenty of money and told me he was in Skegness a couple of days for a conference. He bragged about his high powered job, boasting about the perks and how he travelled to different places all the time, staying in nice hotels.
To me he just seemed like a sad man. This guy had a family but wanted to 'entertain me' in his room. The thought of being anywhere near this old, fat family man repulsed me.

How wrong was this?

He asked me again if I would like to go to his room for a drink. I wanted to shout, 'No way you dirty pervert!'
But, needs must and I decided to take his money, he had plenty and I thought if he wasn't propositioning me he would just go out and pay someone else. I was scared though. It was all too real now.

I gave Colin a nod and as I did I felt a flash of anger that he was letting me even attempt to do this, sleep with another man for money. It had been my decision however, so off we went to the man's room.

He was repulsive, telling me he was happily married with children but that he had 'fun' away from home.

'What the wife doesn't know won't hurt her,' he said following it with a dirty laugh.

I was beginning to feel this really wasn't for me. I felt shocked with myself, ashamed that I was even thinking about doing this. He gave me a drink and asked if he would have to pay to have sex with me. I answered quickly that he would.

I felt sick. I couldn't believe I was contemplating having sex with this disgusting man.

I really didn't want to.

He kissed my neck and I pulled away. I didn't want this dirty, disgusting man putting a finger on me.

He laughed and said 'I guess you are new to all this.'

His dirty laugh really angered me. He knew I was scared but all he cared about was satisfying himself!

All I could think of was getting away, fast.
Burton flashed before my eyes. The same fear and panic welled up and I saw an iron at the side of the bed. Before I knew it, it was in my hand and I had hit him on the head with it.

I didn't know if I had hurt him, nor did I care. I just grabbed his wallet, took the money and ran. Not once looking back to see how hurt he was. He could have been dead for all I knew, it didn't matter.

'Did you do it?' `Colin who was waiting outside asked. I told him I hadn't and then we just ran.

It seemed as if we ran forever. But it was just back to our flat. I told Colin what happened. He got scared and started having a go at me, saying I shouldn't have hit him.

What did he know about how I felt?

And if he did, would he care as long as we had the money?

I had no faith in men especially the way they treated women. Yes, I was happy to take all the man's money. I reasoned that if I had, had sex with him, I would have felt guilty about his wife and family.
Hitting him was the better option.

We decided to go back to the Midlands that very night and very quickly, in case he was badly hurt and the police were looking for us. We were really scared, our minds racing. We got a taxi, which dropped us on the main road leaving Skegness. If the taxi driver thought we were acting oddly, he didn't say so.

After a miserable trip hitching, we finally returned home to the Midlands. In our haste we had left a lot of stuff behind. My father insisted he would go and fetch all our belongings. We didn't go into any details and I let him think we had just fallen out.
He went up to Skegness the very next day to fetch my stuff. I was worried out of my mind.

What if the police were waiting when he got there?
What if they turned up and asked my father where we were?
What if they told him what I had tried to do or told him I had stolen from someone and left them in a bad way?
It was all just so scary, but a few hours later my father arrived home without a problem.

Things were never the same with me and Colin after this and we soon split up. I think fear and shame got the better of us. I never really explained to my parents why moving away hadn't worked out. I decided to keep myself to myself and settle down a bit. I signed up for yet another attempt at college and went for a Youth Training Scheme nursing course.

I still knocked about with the same gang in Uttoxeter. Even though I had been away for a short while all the same faces were there. Most nights, we would meet at the 'five shops' of the little precinct, having the odd drink of cider or whatever one of us could nick from our parents' cupboards and walking to the garage to buy a single fag.

When I was 16 I met Tania, she had just moved onto my road. I hadn't seen her around before but she seemed ok and we started hanging out a lot with each other, spending time round each others houses for tea and listening to music.

By this time my taste in music was changing. I was beginning to love the black music scene and the clubs that went with it like the Blue Note or the Pink Coconut clubs in Derby. Tania got me into this different music. Black, soft music like The Real Thing, Cameo and Cash-flow was what I enjoyed listening to. They were good sounds. The nightlife in Uttoxeter was non-existent. It had one, so called nightclub, the type of place where cheesy DJ's played out-of- date music with a crowd aged 15 to 60.

# **Runaway**

I had started knocking about with an old school friend called Lorna and we spent a lot of time together. I told her I was thinking of going to London and she laughed at the idea, said I must be insane.

It was understandable I suppose. She had never ventured out of Uttoxeter and London seemed a million miles away. We spent a lot of time discussing it, but I think Lorna doubted I would ever really go. But, I could feel the desire for something else burning inside me.

She was wrong.
My mind was made up.
This was going to be a new start.
I was going to London.

I was excited at the prospect of the big city, but frightened at the same time.
I wanted the exciting lifestyle that London offered. The images of our visit to the Royal Albert Hall and shopping in Kensington were still vivid in my mind. I had read about London in magazines of course. I had seen it many times on television. It always looked very glamorous. People always seemed to have lots of money, nice clothes, and flash cars. In my naivety, it seemed that everyone in London lived a celebrity lifestyle. London was everything Uttoxeter was not; exciting, bright and glamorous.

I told Lorna this was it, I was going to London. I still don't think she thought I was going to go through with it. But, in my heart I was already on my way.
She tried to talk through the obvious practicalities.
What was I going to do when I got there?
Where was I going to live?
How would I survive?
Was I going to tell my parents?

I wasn't expecting that last question, had probably been pushing it away.
But, it was the only one I knew the answer to.

My mother and father were not going to be told.

What I was going to do once I arrived in London? I didn't even know which part of London I was going to head for, but I had to take the chance. I really hadn't a clue. But I knew, I just knew, I had to go - there was nothing left for me in Uttoxeter.

I remember thinking at the time, most people living in Uttoxeter must feel the same. They were just too scared to make the move.

For the next week I stayed in at home. Perhaps I hoped things would be different. Different enough to make me want to stay or to make sure I really wanted to leave. I loved my parents very much.
But, it was time to move on and to experience new things.

Lorna was the only person I had confided in. I did feel a pang of guilt that I wasn't going to tell my parents but it was safer if only one person knew. Lorna promised me faithfully she would not say a word. My parents would come looking for me and bring me back home to Staffordshire if they found out.

Much later, I found out that when I disappeared they had been round to her house. She just told them she hadn't seen me for a while and hadn't known I was planning to go anywhere.
She had not betrayed my confidence.
Good old Lorna!

It was a wet and miserable Friday morning when I left, so miserable that leaving Staffordshire seemed even more the right thing to do.
I don't know what sort of climate I was expecting in London.

I waited for my parents to go to work, then quickly rushed to pack a bag, throwing in a couple of pairs of jeans, a couple of tops, a pair of trainers and a few toiletries. I had £50 in my pocket.
I agonised about whether I should leave a note for my parents, but as I didn't know what to say, decided against it.

I checked outside to see if the neighbours were watching. It wasn't as if they would know I was leaving for good, but I didn't want anyone to see me leaving with a bag. Once I had decided the coast was clear, off I went round the block to the bypass. The A50 runs right next to Uttoxeter and it is a major arterial route through Staffordshire. I walked to the petrol station nearby, asking the drivers in the lorries parked there if they were going to London, hoping for a lift. Most of them asked why I wanted to go to London. I was seventeen, and quite obviously young. A couple of them asked me outright if I was running away from home. I quickly told them I wasn't. My story was that I was going to visit friends or relatives, but most of them wouldn't take the chance.

Then one driver said,

'Go on then gal, jump in! Where in London are you heading?'

And I was off.

He was a thick set man of about 50 years of age with a kind face and I felt at ease with him. In hindsight I was stupid for hitch-hiking but then, I really wasn't aware of the dangers. As far as I was concerned, I hadn't got a lot of money and a lift was a lift.

He asked where in London I was off to. I still had no idea about any areas to make for, so asked where he was going. He said he was heading to a place called White City near the old greyhound stadium. I didn't know what he was talking about, but then he mentioned it was close to the BBC headquarters and suddenly, White City seemed very attractive. That would do for starters.
I asked him lots of questions about London. What was it like? What were the people like?

He suggested it would be a good idea if I got the tube from White City to Kings Cross. Accommodation was probably cheaper there than in most parts of London. He told me there were a lot of hostels in the area which catered mainly for Australian and New Zealand students who visited the city on gap years. He also warned me that Kings Cross was a notorious red light area so there would be prostitutes and pimps and drug takers around and that I should be careful.

By this time I think he had gathered that I was running away from home.
It was a long drive up the M1 and finally, he asked me point blank why I was running away.

I didn't know to be honest. And, as I tried to explain it all to him; getting into trouble and being bored didn't seem like very much of a reason.
Nothing was really forcing me to leave and I felt a pang of guilt about my parents.

I enjoyed talking to him. He had been brought up in South London, growing up on a rough estate. He thought I was mad as a hatter to even want to go to London. He had moved up north with his family away from London as soon as he could. As he spoke, I was counting down the distance on the signposts as we got nearer and nearer to London.

The first thing I noticed when we drove through the city was how fast and busy it was. Everything moved at a hundred miles an hour. Everywhere was full of people rushing about with seemingly no time to stop and talk like the folks back home did. I wondered if anyone found friends in this hectic place. Suddenly, London seemed to be very lonely, with no-one knowing anyone else, so very different to Uttoxeter where everyone knew everyone else. It was strikingly different, but exciting at the same time.

We pulled up next to the greyhound stadium at White City. It was all very grey and a bit disappointing really. The driver told me to be careful, to watch what I was doing and as I said goodbye, walking off to goodness knows what, he called me back.

'You can always go back home you know gal, things might seem bad at your age, but in reality nothing is so bad that it can't be patched up with your family,' he said.

I thanked him and assured him I knew what I was doing. I said goodbye once more to this genuinely nice man and set off to the start of my new life.

I walked for a while taking in the surroundings then stopped and stood by the side of the road looking up and down, not knowing what I was going to do. Then, I remembered what the driver had said about heading for Kings Cross; that would be the best option. I went into a paper shop and asked inside how I could get to Kings Cross. I didn't even know where it was or what it was like.

The lady behind the counter said to get the tube at White City, get on the Central Line and change at Oxford Circus, then get on the Victoria Line which went straight to Kings Cross. I had never been on the underground.
It all sounded very confusing.

I soon found out that I didn't like going underground at all. As I went down the escalator I began to panic. 'Pull yourself together,' I told myself.
Amazingly, I managed to get on the right train to Oxford Circus and got off,
stepping into a swirl of people. I felt I was being swept along against my will with the crowd, like a herded animal. I had never seen so many people.
What a crazy place!

There was a mass of tunnels leading to different lines. A guard pointed me to the Victoria Line for Kings Cross. The train was so full I had to stand, which was an experience in itself, with the bumps and swaying all over the place as we thundered through the tunnels. I arrived at Kings Cross not knowing what to expect.

My first impression was not positive. It was very dirty, with homeless people who all seemed to be drunk, lying everywhere. I began to doubt my decision to run away and I now worried if I had enough money. I had spent more than I had bargained for on the tube already and felt lost.
What the hell was I doing?

There was a man standing by the station exit giving out free magazines. I went over and  asked him if he knew where I could find a cheap place to stay. He shoved the magazine toward me grunting. I deciphered that I should have a look in the magazine for accommodation. He was really unfriendly and I realised how lucky I had been with the lorry driver on the way down. It shocked me how rude and unfriendly everyone seemed to be. It was really hitting me how far away I was from home. The man with the papers had seemed almost annoyed I had spoken to him. I grabbed the magazine and found a bench to sit on. The magazine had loads of adverts for Australian hostels, so the lorry driver had been right about that but I had no idea where there were or how to find any of them.

Finally, I saw a kind looking lady at the station ticket office and asked her where the nearest hostel was. She smiled. She had doubtless seen many kids such as me before, landing in London without the first idea where to go or what to do.

Pointing across a very busy main road she said 'If you go past the Wimpy and take the next road on the right, there is a hotel just up there.'

As I walked away she called after me.

'Keep your stuff with you at all times in that place, otherwise it will go missing. And, don't trust anyone!'

Don't trust anyone, I repeated to myself in my head.
I still live by that rule now, even after all these years.

When I got to the hostel it was really busy. The man on the desk said a bed for a week would cost £30 without food. I was a shocked; I don't think I had been living in the real world up to then. I paid him and he showed me to a grotty room with five beds in. There was also a shared kitchen and one shower.

As I was came out of the room to look around, I bumped into a tall blonde girl. She smiled and said hello to me and asked if I would like a drink. I told her I would and she introduced herself as Katy. She was on a working holiday, staying in London until the following week. She began to tell me about her travels. It sounded really exciting. She had travelled round Europe; Paris, Madrid, Rome and now London. Her final stop would be Germany. She would then be returning home to her native South Africa. She was friendly and I admitted to her this was my first day away from home and that I found the whole thing terrifying. She laughed and said I would soon get used to London. She offered me some toast and told me there was always bread for toasting if I wanted any. Money was a worry so I was glad to hear this. At least I could count on having toast for the week.

Katy asked if I wanted to go for a walk round the area so she could show me the various landmarks that would help me get to know the place. We walked out of the hostel and onto the street. I soon noticed quite a few odd looking women standing around. I asked Katy what they were waiting for.

'You are very naïve,' she laughed.

The women were prostitutes, lots of them. They stopped the odd car or passer-by and men approached them. The men then either walked away or scuttled off with

them. Back in Uttoxeter, I thought I was street wise.
In London, I was learning very quickly that I hadn't a clue.

A short distance away, just behind the hostel was a pretty square with flowers and bushes. We just sat for a while watching the working girls try and snare the men. It was fascinating to see. Katy asked what work I was planning to do while I was there. I answered that I didn't know. She suggested bar work might be an idea. There was always a need for bar staff in London. I didn't have any experience of bar work but reasoned it couldn't be all that difficult. Katy informed me that she worked in a local bar herself and invited me to accompany her to work that night to introduce me to her boss, maybe he might have some work for me.

We went back to the hostel. While Katy went to get ready for work I waited for her in the kitchen and had some more toast. She didn't take long and soon we were walking through Kings Cross to where she worked. It turned out to be a really shabby looking back street pub, painted a deep red with blacked out windows. Not the most inviting looking place.

It was as dismal inside as it was out and the hum of loud music I heard as we approached exploded into a din on opening the door.
Katy walked over to an unshaven, scruffy looking man in his 50s. She gave him a hug and introduced him to me as Jon. This was the boss.

Katy said I was new to London and looking for work. Jon looked me up and down, and then asked if I was any good at stripping.

'Stripping?' I repeated.

'Yes love, taking your clothes off.'

I had expected to be asked if I could pull a pint. I tried not to look shocked, then I realised, the 'pub' was a strip-joint.
I told him that wasn't really the sort of work I was looking for; I just wanted normal bar work. He shook his head and said the only thing he had at that moment was a vacancy for a glass-collector. I would have to collect empty glasses while the shows were on. It was easy enough work if I could cope with the occasional grope. It would be seven nights a week starting at six and ending at eleven. For that he would pay me £50 a week.

It would pay for the hostel. I told him I would do it and I tried out for the job that night. The door opened at 5.30 and quite a few men started arriving. Most of them seemed well dressed office types who were calling in before their journey home on the train; a few were regulars and greeted the staff. All the customers, as they came in grabbed chairs and sat as close as possible to the stage.

At 6.30 the strippers appeared and started their routine of dancing and teasing the men who put tips in the last bit of underwear they were wearing. Most of them were very good at what they did and received big tips. Not all of them were good looking, but in the darkish light and with their makeup heavily applied, they looked good enough. Katy pointed a couple of the strippers out and warned me to be careful of them as they were what she termed 'smack-heads'. I wasn't exactly sure what she meant but guessed she was on about heroin as I had seen it on television. I had never actually come across heroin addicts before.

I collected the glasses while the strippers were on, getting the odd suggestive remark or a pat on the bottom as I was working but it wasn't as bad as I thought it would be. At the end of the night Jon came over to me and grunted that I had done alright. He asked if I was interested in the job. I desperately needed the money so I told him I would like the job full-time. It would do for now, I thought.

As Katy and I walked back towards the hostel after we had finished at the pub, I noticed a lot more prostitutes had appeared in the area. It surprised me how old some of them were. But, the place was so alive and animated, so many people around. In Uttoxeter at that time of night you would be lucky to see anyone at all. It seemed to me that no-one ever slept in London.

But, I was getting tired by then. It had been a very strange and very long day. I had runaway, and got myself a place to say and a job in London. I thought of my parents and wondered if they had realised yet that I wasn't coming home.

I went towards a phone-box but decided it would be best not to phone tonight. I was putting it off, I knew, but I couldn't be bothered with an argument or all the questions I would have fired at me if I told them where I was.

The next morning I woke up late. I had slept really well and felt good. I decided to go out for a wander around to see what went on during the day in Kings Cross. Katy wasn't around so I walked around on my own.

It was so grubby in the daylight. There was rubbish on the floor, empty beer cans strewn in doorways, people lying on walls or on the pavement drinking from a large cider bottles.

I went back to the hostel and sat around wondering what to do with myself until it was time to go to work. I felt a lot more relaxed on the second night; the place didn't seem so intimidating. Even Jon almost had a smile on his face. The second night went well and I even got a tip from one of the customers. He said I had a nice smile and gave me some money. I quite enjoyed myself.

The following day Katy said she was meeting a friend for lunch who worked in Covent Garden and asked if I would like to go along with her. I jumped at the chance - I wanted to see more of London. Covent Garden looked very nice to me. It was set in a square, with street entertainers dancing and singing, fire eaters and jugglers. The shops looked expensive with classy clothes, hat shops and expensive hair boutiques.

We met Katy's friend Adrian at a little coffee shop. He was tall, with a mop of blonde hair and really pleasant. He had arrived from Australia a couple of months before. We had lunch in the café and Adrian paid the bill. I was pleased about this as it was very expensive and it would have left me with no money.

Katy suggested we took a walk up to Leicester Square. It was full of theatres, nightclubs, cinemas and quite classy restaurants. It was just so frantic; everywhere we went there were swarms of people. I had never been to such a busy place.

I took an interest in the nightclubs. I thought when I had some money, it would be nice to have a night out and go to one of the clubs, something to look forward to.

We walked through what I later found out was the West End. There were lots of little side streets. I asked Katy where these little streets led to.

'Soho', she said.

We walked up a road called Wardour Street. There were a few shops, one of which was a big Ann Summers shop with loads of dummies in the window dressed in revealing underwear. I wanted to have a look in there but was too embarrassed to tell Katy but I glanced in as we passed. There were all sorts of weird things in there, stuff I'd never seen before.

We were by now in the heart of Soho. There were flashing neon signs everywhere advertising sex shows and 'lovely ladies'. We went past the famous strip-club, Paul Raymond's Review Bar. The place seemed to be throbbing with activity. There were girls on the doors of the clubs shouting out to men to come inside. For a small fee they could spend time with 'beautiful ladies' and see a live sex-show. There were so many doors which were all advertising models. Katy informed me that the 'models' were in fact prostitutes who worked from these little flats. I couldn't believe how alive and lively this area was.

As we walked back up to Oxford Circus, I couldn't get Soho out of my mind, it fascinated me. Then Katy said we should hurry up or we would be late for work.

Work that night was much the same as the night before, a similar mixed crowd of businessmen and locals. I was getting offers to 'spend some time' with a couple of customers after the show. I wasn't interested. Katy looked after me and the rest of the girls were great fun to be around, we had a laugh at the expense of some of the customers and stayed on after hours for a drink. I was enjoying this job

That night when I finished, I walked to the phone box and called my father. I told him I was safe and that I was staying in London. He asked where in London I was but I refused to say. I told him I loved him very much but I wasn't coming home. He reacted a lot better than I expected. He told me that whenever I wanted them or wanted to go home that they would be there for me. It was very emotional talking to him, but I had no intention of going home. I was enjoying myself too much.
The rest of the week went very much the same way and I had some luck with my accommodation. he person who had booked my bed the following week had postponed coming for a month, so I could stay on.

Katy however, was leaving the following morning to carry on with her travels. I think if I had got enough money I might have gone along with her. We worked our last shift together and the girls all bought her a drink.
Then it was time for us to go home.
She had to be up early the next morning and I wouldn't see her again so we had a hug and said our goodbyes there and then. She'd gone when I got up and I suddenly felt very lonely. I was on my own again.

That night, Jon was standing by the door when I got to work and asked me if I would like to try working behind the bar now that Katy had left. He said the customers liked me, then went on to say that I would have to wear more revealing clothes. The men liked to get an eyeful as they were getting served. I said yes, but that I would need teaching how to pour a pint. He laughed and spent a short time showing me the way to pour drinks. With bitter, you had to pour it straight to the bottom of the glass, for the lager you had to tilt as you poured. I picked it up really quickly. The till was easy too. You added the drinks up in your head and then put the money in. No-one would dare steal as Jon had a bit of a reputation for being a nasty and violent man. I had never seen anything to confirm this but I wasn't going to take the chance. I made a couple of little mistakes but nothing major. Jon was pleased and said I had done well. Looking back, I think he had a bit of a soft spot for me. My money went up a little so I could buy a couple of sexier tops.

Dressing sexily wasn't really my thing but after a while I began to like the new me. I was getting lots of compliments, not seedy or sleazy ones and that made me feel more at ease. It became a bit of a running joke that every night, when I went to work Jon would say, 'are you sure you don't want a go at the stripping?' He received the same answer every time, 'no thanks!' I didn't dare, I would have been far too embarrassed.

Life at the hostel and work stayed pretty steady for a while. I started to speak to some of the prostitutes who hung around the area. Most of them did the same spots most nights. They were quite friendly when they got to know your face. They would tell me the occasional story of what they were asked to do or perform with clients. I think they enjoyed telling me because my shocked expression used to make them laugh.

One of them was a black girl called Glynis, who would always stop to chat and ask how I was getting on. She always warned me of the dangers of getting into drugs. If I did, I would probably end up working the streets like she did, she said. She hated working the streets, but had two children and a very big heroin addiction to support. She had worked the streets of Kings Cross for more than ten years and had hated every minute of it. I felt sorry for her but then thought, well why keep taking the drugs if you are so unhappy with your life? I really didn't understand that she took heroin because her life was so unhappy, but her life was unhappy because she took heroin. None of it made sense to me.

Glynis worked alongside another black girl called Martha, who was very tall and slender. We often went into the local Wimpy which was a burger based fast food restaurant chain similar to McDonald's. The one in King's Cross was opposite the train station and was known as a meeting place to score for drugs. It was always full of druggies, prostitutes and strippers buying their drugs after making their money. If it was full around 10.30 you could tell it had been a good night for everyone. You could buy anything in there; hash, amphetamine, cocaine or heroin. Cocaine was not a big drug in the mid 80s. It was just too expensive back then. Most people that went in to buy drugs were after heroin. It did seem at times as if everyone in London took some kind of drug. I started smoking weed with Glynis and Martha. They would often have one lit up as I passed them on my way home after work. I had smoked weed before but was never that bothered about it. If it was passed around then I would have a quick smoke but I would never go and buy it.

I later found out that Martha was a man who was saving for a sex change operation. She had also been around for years and said she only worked for her operation money, but with her big heroin problem I couldn't see how she would ever manage to save up enough for it. The two of them together were really funny, with their mad stories of the things men asked them for. One of Martha's regular businessmen clients liked her to dress him up like a big baby, and then feed him with a giant baby's bottle that he kept in his briefcase. I was sometimes dubious about whether the stories were all true, They used to laugh at my disbelief, calling me 'little Miss Innocent'. And, if the stories were made up, they were very convincingly told.

I used to see Glynis every night when she worked the road next to the Wimpy. One night as we walked back up the road, she showed me the place where they took the men for sex. It was a traditional London square with a bit of a park in the middle enclosed by shrubbery.

As we were walking through we got stopped by the police. Glynis was asked if she was out working that night, she said she wasn't and had just met me, her friend, from work and we were walking home. The police just laughed and gave her a ticket with a warning on it which said that if she was seen in the same area again that same night she would be arrested for soliciting.

They turned to me and asked if I was new to 'the Cross'. I said I was and that I worked in a local pub. The two policemen looked at each other and then shook there heads.

'Another one to look out for,' one of them said.

I protested that I wasn't a prostitute but they wouldn't listen. They gave me the same ticket they had given Glynis. Angrily, I kept trying to make them understand I wasn't a prostitute. I even offered to take them to the bar where I worked to prove it. They just laughed and told me that if I didn't move on they would take me in to the station.

Glynis was annoyed, she had only just come out to work, so she was going to take her chances and stay out, just ducking if she saw any police. This kind of thing happened all the time and was all in a nights work for her. It was a hazard of the job, a battle of wits between prostitutes and the law.

I hadn't left the Cross apart from the couple of times I had gone into the West End with Katy. One morning, with nothing to do, I decided to go out for a wander around. I vaguely remembered how to get to Covent Garden so thought I would go and see if Katy's friend, Adrian, was still working at the Body Shop there. I got the tube to Oxford Circus and walked to Covent Garden and the Body Shop and asked if Adrian was working. He wasn't, like Katy he had carried on travelling.

My intention had been to take him out to lunch to repay him for the one he had bought me and Katy the first time we met, and now I was at a loss.
I got a coffee and sat there wondering what to do and where to go. I remembered Soho and how it had fascinated me the first time I saw it with Katy.

It was as busy as I remembered from that first visit. People rushing around and others standing around looking at the girls in the doorways. It had the same effect on me again, fascination. I wandered around the area just watching how things worked. I saw the girls capture men and disappear into the clubs.
I wondered what really went on there; did they actually see a real sex show?

I walked down a street called Frith Street. There was a big shop front with a little desk just set back. Bright neon signs advertised live sex shows.
The name of the club, Maximillian's, made me chuckle, being so similar to my own name. A big foreign looking man on the door was looking straight at me. I looked away, but when I glanced again he hadn't taken his eyes off me. I thought he had

kind eyes and I didn't feel uncomfortable at all. He was tall and his face was framed with a big beard. I thought he looked friendly.

I saw him call a man over. I couldn't hear what he was saying but the man paid him and disappeared down the stairs into the club.

The big man's gaze returned to me and he called me over. I hesitated. Unsure, I looked around, there was no-one else near. It was me he was calling.

I don't know why, but I took off. I ran all the way back to the tube station. When I got on the train, breathless, I felt stupid for running away without even knowing what he was going to say. I sat there, annoyed with myself all the way home.

I got ready for work back at the hostel, still annoyed, and all through the shift I kept thinking about Soho and the big bearded man on the door of the club. After work, I met up with Glynis and Martha. Glynis seemed upset about something. When I asked her if anything was wrong she said she didn't want to talk about it. I told them about my running away experience that afternoon and they had a bit of a chuckle at me and Glynis cheered up a little. They said I should go back the next day and find out what he wanted.
I wasn't so sure.

The next day as I got up and looked out the window, the traffic was as normal, bumper to bumper with the occasional beeping of horns, the business people rushed around to get their trains but everything seemed muted. Something was different, something amiss, something I couldn't quite put my finger on.

I walked in the rain to the Wimpy for coffee. As usual a couple of street girls were in there. They asked if I knew Glynis.

'Yes,' I replied, 'she was with me last night after work.'

I told them I had left her in the Wimpy with Martha. Both the girls looked down at the floor and then one said Glynis had taken a huge overdose of heroin and was dead. Her body had been found that morning in the park area at the back of the hostel. The police hadn't established yet what time she had died.
I had sensed there had been something wrong the night before. Now I was in shock. I agonised that maybe if I hadn't left her in the Wimpy it might not have happened. Whys? And What ifs? rushed through my head.

Before I could collect my thoughts, Martha came through the door. She was devastated. They had been so close, working side by side for so many years, watching over each other.
She asked if she could come up to the hostel for a while, so I took her back there

and made us a drink. Martha said the reason Glynis had been so upset last night was because she had been told that morning that her children were being taken away from her. Her heroin addiction meant she wasn't providing for them properly and she was leaving them alone at night while she worked.

We never got to hear when or where Glynis's funeral was to be held, which was quite sad. I would guess her family didn't want her 'street-friends' anywhere near the service.

I saw Martha shortly afterwards. She had been told only Glynis's children and Mother were there on the day. The rest of the family could not forgive her for her lifestyle. They couldn't understand why she couldn't get off the drugs and get help to sort her life out. It was all so sad but it seemed like that it was quite the norm for London.

I didn't see much of Martha after Glynis died. She couldn't work Kings Cross without her friend and moved on. I heard later that she was taking more heroin than ever and was not in the best of health. I saw her occasionally and she always looked awful. Her skin was in a bad way and she was dirty, thin and drawn.

The last time I saw her, she was still saving for her sex-change operation.

# Soho

I had become friends with a couple of lads who hung around the area. They were rent-boys. When they told me they were rent-boys, I thought they meant that they collected rent from tenants and wondered why they would be in the Wimpy. I told them this and they burst out laughing finding my naivety funny, but they explained what rent-boys did. They hung around the station, where they would pick up men who wanted sex with them, at a price of course.

I knew them as Robbie and Tom, probably not their real names. I didn't think until I met them, that men did that sort of thing. I had never really thought about it before. Back in Uttoxeter I didn't know anyone who was gay. Robbie and Tom weren't, and occasionally, they popped into the bar where I worked for a beer and a look at the ladies. They sold their bodies to gay men for drug money.

One night in the pub, there was a crowd of city boys in, brokers and traders, who were being a bit of a nuisance, grabbing at the strippers. A doorman explained that the girls were not to be touched. One of them didn't like this and started pushing the doorman. They were told to leave. I expected a big scene, but they just got up and walked out. However, half an hour later a window was smashed in. The doorman ran outside to see what had happened but there was no one to be seen.

Later, as I was walking back to the hostel, a couple of the city boys were still hanging around. I was a bit nervous but carried on. They started to follow me.
I walked faster. So did they. At last, I got to the Wimpy and ducked in quickly, hoping that someone I knew would be in and luckily there was a couple of dealers that I did know. I told them what had happened and about being followed. They went straight out and confronted the men that had followed me. There was a lot of shouting but the city boys didn't fancy it and walked away. It was frightening. I didn't know what they planned to do to me and it made me realise the dangers of the job and being alone in the area.

The next day I walked up to Soho. It was as busy as it had been before. I called into the Ann Summers shop that had intrigued me so much. Some of the stuff in the shop; well I wouldn't even know what to do with most of it, but I did buy some nice underwear. I have always liked nice underwear.

Pleased with my purchase, I carried on wandering around Soho. There was a

market with stalls selling fruit and vegetables, stalls selling clothes, jewellery and bits and bobs. The market epitomised the mixed character of Soho.
There were the everyday normalities of life; markets, schools, shops and people living in and around Soho happily existing alongside the drug trade, and the blatantly advertised sex and sleaze which was everywhere you looked. The shops were nothing like I had seen before in Uttoxeter. One shop was called Zeitgeist, selling rubber dresses, trousers and skirts. There was a big shop called Boy which had amazing clothes and shoes.
This place just fascinated me.

There was such a variety of people, the door girls, the street workers and the men looking for ladies or shows. And then children, going to and from school or to the market, walking through them all.
It was captivating.

I walked up Wardour Street to Frith Street where the club Maximillian's was. There was a dark haired girl on the door this time. The bearded man was there but he was standing across the road with another man who was very tall.

The bearded man saw me and he smiled and called me over. This time I didn't run away like an idiot but walked straight up to them. He asked if I worked in Soho, I said I worked in a bar in Kings Cross. He said they were looking for young, attractive girls to work the doors, and would I like to try working in his club. I must have looked nervous as the tall man suggested I went for coffee with them. 'I'll tell you all about the job,' he said as we walked down the street to a little Italian coffee bar.

The man spoke with a foreign accent. I asked were he was from and he said he was from Malta and his name was Mario. He was a partner in the club. He introduced the bearded man as Dougie. The job entailed me sitting on the door calling out to passing men, telling them there were ladies inside and a very sexy show. I would make £3 for every man I sent downstairs. He asked if I would like to go back to the club and have a look inside and meet the girls. I said yes I would have a look. My legs were shaking and I felt really nervous. I'm not sure why. Whether it was meeting new people or that I was going into the unknown.

I walked into the club and the dark haired girl who I had seen earlier on the door said hello to me. She introduced herself as Scottish Jack. She was very slim, with long dark hair and seemed pleasant enough. Mario asked her if there were any men downstairs. She shook her head so he gestured that we should go inside. We went down some stairs. It was dark with a few lights giving the staircase a red glow. Reaching the bottom of the stairs, I was shocked at the size of the place.

It was huge, with a bed in the middle of the room. Off to the side there were little cubicles. Each one had a sofa and a table with a candle in the middle of it. Around

the bed there were other sofas. The whole place was surprisingly well decorated with black and silver wallpaper and pictures on the walls.
I really couldn't believe how big it was.

As I looked round, I noticed a big counter built into the wall. There was a pretty blonde girl sat behind the counter reading a book. Mario walked over to the counter and spoke to the girl.

'Rene, this is Maxine, she is going to be our new door girl.'

The girl looked up and greeted me in a broad Scottish accent,

'Hi Maxine,' she said as she offered me her hand to shake,

'Do you fancy a bottle of Holsten Pils?'

I looked down and there was a crate of beer on the floor.

Rene grinned at me and said, 'They're all mine, the beer for punters is in the fridge.'

I had a beer with her and we talked for a while. She told me she had a son to Dougie and had worked in Soho for eight years. We were getting on really well but suddenly I realised the time and that I had to get to work. I said my goodbyes and Mario asked if I wanted the job and if I did, when could I start.
I told him the following day but I would only work the morning shift which finished at three o'clock. He smiled and said that was fine then gave me a hug. I rushed to the tube station and just about made it in time for work.

I decided not to mention Soho to Jon or any of the girls in case I didn't like it or it didn't work out. The same old faces greeted me as I walked towards the bar. It was a normal night with the usual punters sat at the bar.

After work, I walked up to the Wimpy to see if Martha was around to tell her about Soho, the club and the job offer. I wanted to get her opinion but she wasn't about. Robbie and Tom were however, so I went in, grabbed a coffee and joined them at a table. I told them all about Maximillian's and asked what they thought. Robbie said he had worked Soho before but the police had got to know him too well and he had been forced to move to the Cross. He did say there was a good chance to make decent money there, more than the pittance I was being paid in the pub.

Robbie reckoned that within a week of working Soho I would pack in my job at the bar in Kings Cross. Just the difference in money alone would persuade me that it wasn't worth my while working in the bar. He said the Soho crowd were good fun, they all looked out for each other a bit like one big family. I don't think I quite understood what he meant by that but I didn't ask. I would just wait and see for myself.

They said they had to go out to earn some money themselves, wished me the best of luck with my new job and left. Time was getting on, so I thought it would be good to get an early night for my big debut in Soho the next morning. I was getting very nervous about the whole thing now. I remember worrying that I would be hopeless at the job. What would happen if I couldn't get anyone to come into the club? I suddenly realised it would all be down to me. I made myself a drink and climbed into bed still wondering if I would be alright and fell asleep, dreaming of my big day in Soho.

# The Switch

It was my first day working in the heart of Soho. I walked up to the doors of Maximillian's and took a deep breath, I was so nervous but I hoped it wouldn't show. The big bearded man was on the door chatting to a smaller man who looked Maltese. They both greeted me. The bearded man, Dougie introduced the little man Bop. Bop was the third partner in the business. Bop looked a little bit like George Michael and was very funny. Dougie asked me if I wanted a hot chocolate. 'Doing the door' as it was known as, was a cold job. The door area was open to the elements. There was a small counter which had a much need small fan heater behind it.

The counter was at the front, just slightly set back; next to it was a little corridor with stairs going down. There was a tiny shop at the back selling videos and books. A curtain prevented the public seeing browsers. The place was quite nicely decorated upstairs, not scruffy at all. The colour scheme was black and silver here too and I noticed the wallpaper had the head of Marilyn Monroe in the pattern.

Dougie came back with the hot chocolate. I sat behind the desk and music suddenly blared out. I think it was Cher or something similar, to entice men to come into the club. I was very nervous and struggled with calling out 'live show' to everyone who passed by. Dougie came out and said I needed to be a bit louder. He also told me to be very careful not to call if the police were in the area, as they would arrest me. Apparently they could charge me with 'obstruction of the Queen's highway'. It was only a small fine, but if you were charged three or more times with it they could make it a prison sentence. That made me even more nervous! I sat there calling to passers-by without much success.

I was getting fed up; I was cold and not making any money. Then, out of nowhere, a little Japanese man arrived. He didn't ask any questions, just gave me the money. I pressed a little button that told the girls there was a customer on their way and he went downstairs. I was inquisitive as to how it worked downstairs but didn't have the nerve to go and look for myself. It would mean I would have to leave the door, so I stayed where I was. Once I had got the first customer, they all seemed to want to come in. My confidence grew, I was buzzing. The Japanese man left. He didn't say a word. No-one did really, customers rarely spoke.

Another thing I immediately noticed was that there was no 'typical' punter. You couldn't say there was a certain look for a potential customer because they were all so different. As I sent another one in through the door, I checked the money situation. I had already earned £70! I couldn't believe it. That was a fortune to me compared to the £50 a week I was getting at the pub. And, my shift wasn't over yet. After a while I needed the ladies which was downstairs. I called out to Dougie and told him.

He sat on the door for me while I popped downstairs. When I arrived downstairs I noticed Rene was there, working, with a tall thin girl. They shouted over to me.

'You are doing a brilliant job on that door Max. We want you on all our shifts!'

I wasn't sure what she meant at the time but thanked her anyway.

I went back up on the door calling the punters in. I was promising them 'live ladies' and 'sexy shows!' It was near the end of my shift. Dougie came out to talk to me. He reminded me of a big bear. Dougie told me in broken English that I had done very well. The girls were happy downstairs as I had made them a lot of money. The punters had been good. There had been no hassle and there had been lots of punters in. The bar had taken £5000. The girls got 27% of that. No wonder they were happy. I had made good money; it seemed too good to be true. Dougie said that I should leave the door then as the other door person would take over. He suggested that I went downstairs to meet the girls and get to know them.

Downstairs, Rene had her usual crate of Holsten Pils and offered me one straight away.

'Get this down you, you've done very well,' she said.

She called the other girl I had seen earlier over and introduced her as Sadie. Sadie was tall and slim with short dark hair. She told me she and her sister had worked in Soho for about a year. Before that she had worked and lived in Saudi Arabia for a while. Rene was married to Dougie. They had a son and they lived in East London. She asked where I lived and I told her it was a hostel in Kings Cross. She nearly choked on her beer when I said that.

'My god! Why do you live there? 'It's a shit hole! You need to find somewhere round here.'

I related how I had left home with £50 in my pocket and that the hostel was the cheapest I could find. Rene had been in London since she was fifteen. Her family had moved from Inverness in Scotland to Corby in Northamptonshire when she was 13 with British Steel. Her elder sister had gone to London and Rene had followed her to Soho, their younger sister followed them both and now all three worked in different clubs. We sat and chatted a while and I told them about Uttoxeter.

They laughed when I said what it was like. They asked if I was a farmer's girl. I laughed and said no. As we were chatting, a buzzer sounded. I asked Rene if she wanted me to disappear.

'No', she said. 'Watch and learn what goes on.'

The punter came down the stairs and Sadie took his ticket from him. She asked if he would like to sit down and he wandered over to a seat close to the stage. Sadie asked if he would like a drink and then got him the small beer he wanted from Rene at the bar.

Sadie then offered him her company. He said no, but told her that he liked the look of Rene. Rene walked over with a cocktail in her hand and sat down next to him. He was only allowed to talk to her, not touch. They spoke for a short while. She asked him about himself, his work, his family and what he liked to do in his spare-time.

After around five minutes, Sadie took the bill over. The man looked at it and jumped, yelling that he hadn't got that much money. Sadie pushed him back onto the chair and told him to start looking for it in his wallet or his bill would go up further, for time wasting. The man was shaking and started to cry. He pulled his wallet out to pay the bill. It was £170. He only had about £130 of it. Sadie said he had to show her identification and then go to the bank to get the remainder of the bill.

Sadie had written all his details down on the back of the bill. It was intended to scare him. Rene had already found out he was married, so the chances of him returning to pay the rest were good. I just couldn't believe how easy it all was.

While he was out fetching the remainder of the money, I asked them what he would get to see when he returned to see the 'sexy show'. They laughed and said that the punters usually ran back in, paid the bill, got their details back and left. They normally left without actually seeing anything.

After about 10 minutes the buzzer went again. This time it was a different man. Sadie approached him and showed him to a seat. He ordered a drink and said he would like her company. They didn't take the bill over straight away. I asked why they hadn't this time. Rene said because if they did and he kicked off, the other man might come back at the same time. If they ganged up together and called the police, we could lose all the money.

The buzzer went again. The girls were right; it was the first punter with the remainder of the money. As they said, he paid up and left very quickly. After he had left, Rene took the bill straight over to Sadie's punter. He sent her away, saying he would like to buy Sadie another cocktail. Rene let them chat for a while longer, then presented him with a bill for £230 and he paid it straight away. He also bought Rene a drink. It all seemed like madness to me. He had been in the club all of twenty minutes and he had spent over £300. Rene buzzed for Dougie to come down into the club. She whispered to Dougie that the man had plenty of 'floose', which was Maltese for money.

Dougie presented the man with yet another bill and told him he had to settle up before the sex-show started. The man looked confused, as he had already paid for the drinks but Dougie told him it was a 'booking-fee' for the two ladies he had sat with. Dougie completely made up a fee of £200 for the two ladies promised and the punter paid it. This wasn't even in the price-list. It was whatever they thought the punter had left. The customer asked when the show would start. Sadie said in around 30 minutes. The punter finished his drink and left saying he hadn't got the time to wait. Sadie gave him a free pass to come back at another time. He left looking really happy.
I thought I was seeing things.

Sadie and Rene were very happy. They laughed at the shock on my face.

I said to Rene, that I couldn't believe it! He had just paid £500 and left without seeing anything. They laughed again, saying that's how it worked.

It was time for me to go. I said goodbye to Rene and Sadie and went upstairs. I wanted to find out when or if they wanted me to work again. Dougie said he most definitely did want me to work again. He offered me all the morning shifts apart from Saturday which someone else already worked.

I got the tube back to Kings Cross and the hostel and counted my money. I had been paid £110 for one morning shift! That was almost a week's wages for a half-decent job in the 80s. I decided I would still go to work at the pub, even though the money I had earned in one day at Maximillian's was more than I could get in a week there. I didn't like letting people down.

I was on a high that night at work. I just couldn't get my head around the workings of Soho. I couldn't believe how stupid men were to pay out all that money. It was literally money for nothing. If they came to the pub I was working in that night, they would pay normal pub prices and watch full strips. All they were expected to give was a small tip to the strippers.

On my way home I went looking for Martha. I found her standing on one street corner. She looked truly awful, out of her face on heroin. I managed to get her to go for a coffee with me. I told her all about Soho and she said I should get out of the Cross as fast as I could.

I felt so sorry for this mixed up person. She was the wrong sex, she hated herself

for that and I couldn't see her ever managing to afford the change from man to woman, I thought she would probably die the same way as Glynis had before she would manage to sort her life out. It was so sad watching her torture herself night and day.
She was so down; still struggling with Glynis's death.

She said she was going to try and get on a drug programme to get clean. I knew it was all just talk, it would never happen. I had listened to other drug users talking in the Wimpy before. Most only went on programmes when they got caught. It wasn't that they wanted to get off the drugs. It just meant their prison sentence was reduced if they agreed to go on those sorts of programmes. As soon as they were out of prison they were straight back on the streets and the heroin. It was a game to most of them.

I stayed with Martha a little longer, talking about Soho and life in general. When we said our goodbyes, Martha went off into the night to earn more drug money and I went back to the hostel and got a good night's sleep in readiness for my second encounter with the West End.

I travelled to work at Maximillian's on the tube. How I hated the tube. You were all cramped up, standing next to some sweaty person. Everyone was rushing about here and there. I consoled myself at the prospect of having a good shift that morning like the day before. If I did, I would get a taxi home. I got to work a little early. In those days I didn't like being late for anything. The shutters were still down in front of the doors and windows so I went to the little Italian coffee shop that Dougie had got my hot chocolate from. It was a really tiny shop which had a long, thin counter and tall stools. There were boxing gloves hanging up on the walls. I had a look at them, they were signed by Rocky Marciano.

It was a friendly place. The two guys behind the counter said,

'You must be the new girl who works for Dougie and Mario'.

That surprised me a little but I said that I was. By the time I had finished and then walked back up Frith Street to Maximillian's, the shutters were up and the music was playing, I found Mario inside and we had a little chat. Then I went and sat at the door to begin my shift. The music was Diana Ross; punters were going in and out of the shop part of the club. They left carrying little brown bags. They didn't even look at me; it was like they wanted to get in and out unseen by anyone.

Then suddenly Bingo! I managed to get my first punter in. He was a little German man. As he trotted downstairs I pressed the buzzer to let the girls know he was on his way down. Ten minutes later he came stomping up the stairs looking very upset. He told me in broken English that I was a liar. He said the people downstairs had stolen all his money. I felt nervous at this stage, not sure what to say. I asked if he had agreed for the lady to sit with him. He shouted that he had. I said he would have only paid for what he had received. That didn't placate him, he was getting angrier. I thought he was going to hit me at one point. Then he suddenly shook his head, swore at me in German and stomped away. He didn't go far. Just as I was getting someone else to come into the club, he shouted that we were all crooks in there. The potential customer changed his mind. The German looked pleased that he had stopped someone else being fleeced and satisfied, he moved on.

I was taken aback by the whole episode. The job obviously wasn't as easy as I had thought. It was the first time I had to deal with irate customers after they had been ripped off and realised that part of the job wasn't that easy.

As the German had finished his last shout and disappeared, a small curly haired girl ran upstairs. She wanted to know if I was alright. I hadn't met this girl yet. She introduced herself as Maggie.

She looked like a mini-Madonna and had curls bouncing everywhere. I said I was alright and she bounced back down the stairs singing as she went. The next few punters were no trouble. One refused a drink and was asked to leave straight away. It stated on the menu in small print - one drink must be purchased to see a show.

I then had a very odd experience. A man and woman approached the club asking about the show. I was a bit taken aback as I didn't think for a minute a woman would wander in to see a show. It was quite strange. The woman was about 50 and very well dressed, like a City business woman. She looked out of place but it was her that did all the talking. I'm sure her partner wasn't that interested, seeming to be there just for her sake. I let them in.

They went downstairs and ordered drinks. Much to the surprise of the girls downstairs, the woman agreed to Maggie's company when she offered. Later they told me they hardly ever had women in the club, they were as shocked as I was.

The man paid the bill and the couple watched a show. She was apparently far more interested in it than the man. She also asked for a private strip, which on occasion, if the coast was clear, was allowed. There was a back room that was used as a changing room and the girls sometimes did a private dance and strip there for a good price.

It was only the top half that punters got to see. The whole thing took just the length of a single record and most of that was dancing. When she had seen the show they came back up. Her partner hadn't spoken the whole time they were downstairs. As they left, she thanked me for the nice ladies. I found the couple very creepy. It didn't seem right to me. I thought of my own mother and could never imagine that she would ever dream of entering a place like this.

Maggie came bounding up the stairs. She was laughing and giggling about the odd couple. She said the woman had just ordered her partner to pay and he had, even when she demanded a private show.

Maggie asked if I fancied a quick break from the door. I said yes and popped downstairs. When I went back up, Maggie was standing there dressed in fishnets, black bra, knickers and high heels, completely unfazed that she was wearing only underwear. She asked if I had been in Soho long as she hadn't seen me before and I said it was only my second day. She then invited me to go for a drink with her and Rene to meet some people from different clubs. It sounded good to me so I agreed.

We had a few more punters in the club spending silly money. The girls and the bosses were pleased, the takings were good and we had all made a good amount. After work, I phoned the pub to say I couldn't work that night.

I was going to go out with the girls around Soho. It was a bit strange working here then going out drinking in the same place with the same people. Martha and Glynis had been right; it was like a little family.
The first pub we went into was called The Intrepid Fox on Wardour Street. It was a strange gothic looking pub with netting on the ceiling and fly posters on the walls, advertising live gigs from way back to the present day. The Clash and the Sex Pistols blasted out of the speakers. This was my sort of bar I thought. The barmen were punks and one of them had the biggest red Mohican I had ever seen. It was just so cool. This was the pub to be seen in if you were in a band or wanted to be. The place was so busy, the atmosphere so exciting. Everyone seemed to know everyone.

A large, very good looking lad came over and picked Maggie up and swung her round. He had a mass of dark curly hair right down his back. Maggie squealed that it was Don, her brother. A broad Glaswegian accent boomed out a hello as he shook my hand.

We left the Fox after a couple of drinks then headed into the heart of Soho and up Great Windmill Street passing quite a few clubs on the way. Maggie stopped at them all introducing me to the other girls who worked the doors.

Rene left us at one club so she could pop in and see her sister, but said she would meet us at the Red Lion. The Red Lion was on a corner of Great Windmill Street. There was a club opposite called the Pink Pussycat and one to the side of it called The Windmill. The Windmill was run by a couple of black guys. Maggie said it was only smack heads who would work there, and it was rough as hell.

The Red Lion was a normal looking bar. There was a black guy standing by the door, looking out of the window towards the clubs. Maggie gave him a hug and introduced us. His name was Duke and he was one of the lads who owned the

Windmill. He smiled at me then asked Maggie if I was looking for work. Maggie laughed at him and said,

'Like I would let an innocent nice girl work for you lot!'

Duke laughed at that and said it was worth a try and bought us a drink.

Soon, Rene came in with the short-haired girl, Sadie, who I had met on the first day. They told me a bit about Soho and working in the clubs. Rene said the main thing to be wary of was if a punter came back with the police. Her sister had been through a court case recently. A punter had entered and paid the bill, he had even watched the show. Then when the show was over, he had gone out on to the streets looking for a policeman to report what had happened. Unluckily for her, he was English with no marital ties or work commitments. He told the policeman that he had been robbed in the club for services he didn't understand he would have to pay for.

She was charged with demanding money with menaces, blackmail and robbery. Luckily, he dropped the charges at the last minute and she was free to walk away. Both Sadie and Rene had worked that shift and said they couldn't believe he came back with the police. He didn't complain once about the bill, he had just paid it, sat through a show and even tipped the show girl.

The other thing to watch for was a certain grey-bearded policeman who despised anyone who worked in Soho. He would arrest people for anything, but his favourite targets were the door-girls. They warned me that he would hide, and then when you called out 'live show' he would pounce and arrest you straight away for highway obstruction.

Highway obstruction was a ridiculous charge. Basically, if a punter stopped to read the menu on the door, or you called out and a punter stopped to listen to what you had to say, he or she was obstructing the highway. I still can't work this charge out because if that is right everybody window shopping on Oxford Street, especially at Christmas, could be arrested for blocking the pavement in the same manner.

I did try and say this later on in Soho, when I got arrested for that offence but the police just laughed at me. It was just a way of getting us to stop what we were doing. But, of course it didn't.
As Rene and I were chatting, a tall thin girl walked in, got a drink and sat down to join us, it was Rene's best friend Wanda, who worked at a big club we had passed earlier called Erotica.

She had very long legs and was wearing the shortest skirt I had ever seen. As she drank a neat vodka she told us she had been to see her 'Daddy' who looked after her, I must've looked a little confused. Rene and Wanda started laughing at my

*Early picture, enjoying myself at fair.*

*Wearing one of my infamous 'Miss Mouse' dresses.*

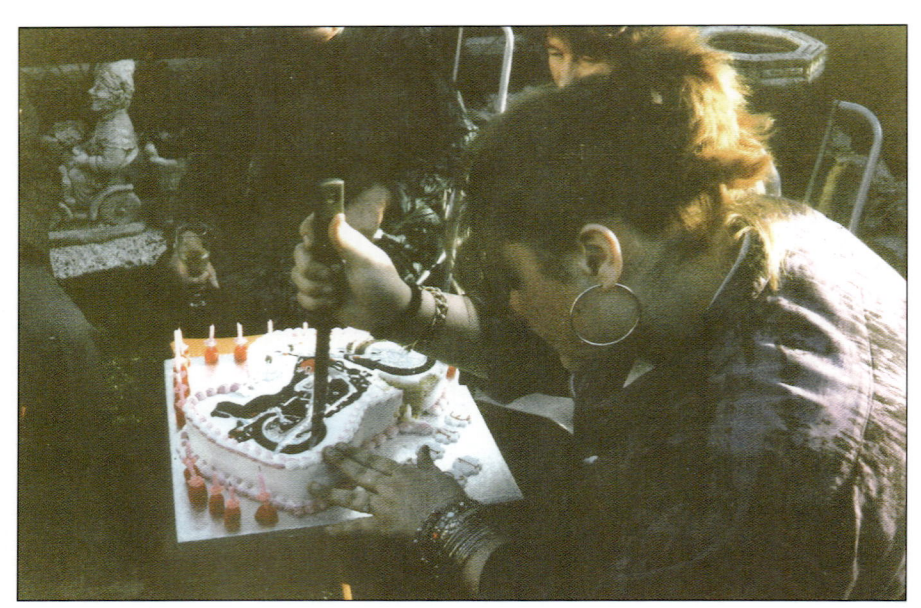

*My Birthday with motorbike themed cake.*

*Showing the signs of my ill-gotten-gains. Outfit courtesy of shoplifting spree.*

*Trip to London in my early teens.*

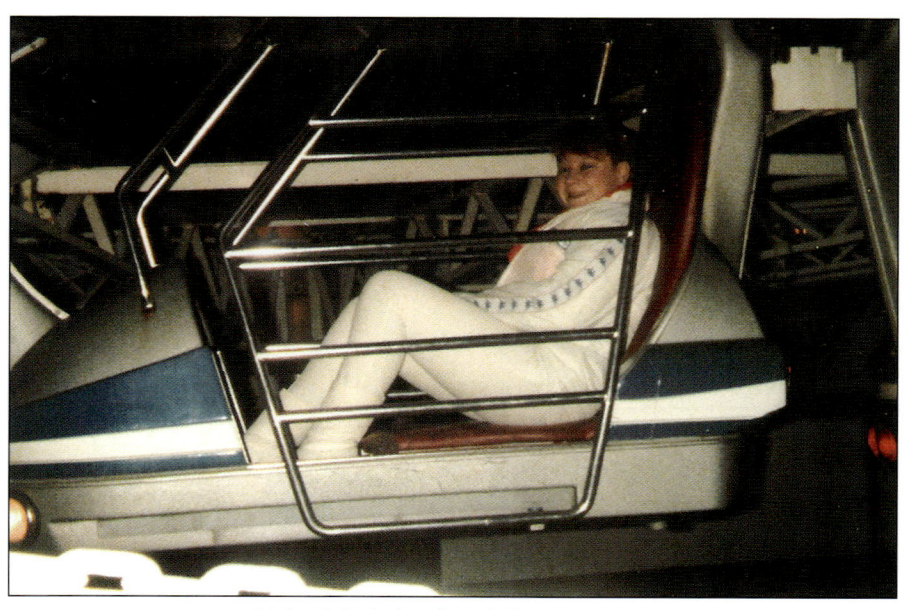

*At the fair during Break Dancing days.*

*My first Soho flat above Little Ade's pink flat.*

*The now defunct Intrepid Fox on Wardour St, Soho.*

*Inset: The first floor windows of the Intrepid Fax gave a good panoramic view of the immediate area.*

expression. Then, Wanda lifted her top up and showed us her back. I was so shocked. It was welts and bruises from top to bottom.

She sat down and said she had an old man who was a punter and an old family friend who, once a month, paid her £400 to take a beating. It 'only' lasted around 30 minutes. He would whip her, or use a belt, but only on her back. That was his enjoyment. He had asked her if she could take a friend next time and was prepared to make it £1000 for two girls so he could beat them together. She asked Rene if she would be interested in what she called easy money. Rene said not a chance and we all shook our heads when she looked at us.

This was all a bit strange to me. I had never heard anything like this.

Wanda was having two drinks to our one, talking about various punters she had served over the years. Maggie told us about an American she once had in Erotica, who had gone in and sat down, buying her cocktail after cocktail. Maggie wasn't hopeful as Americans didn't have the best name in Soho as it was always really hard to get them to pay. They usually ran out of the club screaming or hitting out at the girls to escape. This one however was happy to have Maggie sat with him, only Maggie; he wouldn't have another girl join them.

Rene's sister, Cassandra, or Cass as we knew her, was at the bar and as she took the bill over, everyone expected him to do a runner, but he paid his bill, no problem. Then he asked Cass if the girls liked to wear leather as that was his fetish. Cass said 'Oh yes! We are all into leather but if you want to see us in it you will have to take us shopping to get some.' The American smiled and said he would like to, as money was no object to him, but again, he would only take Maggie. Maggie agreed to go and when they left, Cass nipped outside to get one of the Maltese to follow them, just in case this guy attacked Maggie as he seemed quite obsessed by her.

But, he was true to his word. In those days Soho had lots of leather shops. Maggie took him into one and he wanted her to have a tasselled leather mini with a bra to match. He also treated all the girls who were working that shift to a leather jacket each.

Maggie couldn't believe it, he paid the bill and they went back to the club and she dressed up in front of him, telling him the whole time what the leather felt like on her skin and how sexy and domineering she felt while putting it on.

Then he said, 'Please Miss, may I use the toilet?' When she said he could, he went into the toilet for a short while then left the club. The girls were very happy with their jackets and the £3500 bill he had paid. I asked if she had many punters like this. She said on occasion you would get what they called a 'diamond'.

Eventually, I had taken in so much information about Soho I was exhausted and said I had better be getting home. The others were going to go to a club and suggested I hailed a taxi as it was late. We hugged our goodbyes and I went on back to the hostel.

The next day on my shift, a dark skinned man came up to me. He looked mixed-race or Asian. He chatted for a few minutes then all hell broke loose. A van pulled up and twenty or so men jumped out. It frightened the life out of me. Dougie came charging out of the shop and yelled at me not to worry, it was just a police raid on the shop part of the business.

The man who had spoken to me told me to leave the door and go downstairs with the others to be questioned. I wondered why they wanted to question me as I only sat on the door.

The raid seemed to last for ages, with plainclothes police running about looking for hidden video's and magazines. They opened a door I had not even noticed before. I was told this led all the way to tunnels which went through the West End. Most of the clubs were connected through an underground maze of tunnels. If one club got raided you could bet the rest knew about it in minutes.

The same policeman came over to question us all, he was asking what we thought they sold in the shop, where they hid the stock and if we ever watched the video's or sold them. It was pointless as most of us had no idea what happened in the shop.

When the raid had finished, the police disappeared as quickly as they had appeared, taking bags of video tapes they had found, Dougie said we had done well as we had all kept calm. Everything they had taken would be returned the next day as there was nothing on any of the tapes that was against the law. Then he winked and said,

'That's it now for at least a month, now I can get the proper tapes out'.

I was learning different things every day about the goings on in Soho. The door to the tunnels all over Soho amazed me and I asked if I could go in there. Dougie laughed and said he would get the showman who was called Mark to give me a guided tour one day.

With all the excitement over I went back to the door and started calling out to punters

'Live show, sexy ladies!'

The punters started to come in and it was business as usual again. Rene was doing the bar and I asked her to ask around for a room or flat that I could rent. She said one of the girls her sister worked with was looking for someone to rent a room.

Apparently she was very laid back, easy going and very trustworthy. She would go and see her after work

Things were going so well at that time. I was happier than I had been for ages. I had been working in Soho for less than a week but felt so at home. I just seemed to fit into the way things worked. The lifestyle was so exciting; no day was ever the same as another.

As I was finishing my shift, a red haired man with a big beard came to the door. I asked him if he would like to see the show, he laughed.

'Oh no my dear. I'm here to see Rene. I am Jack, her brother-in-law.'

I buzzed down and Rene came running upstairs. She asked if I was alright, then she saw Jack. He said he was just passing and wanted to know if she was going to the Red Lion after work for a drink. She said she was but after she had seen her friend Dora to ask about a room for me.

After he left Rene told me he was what's known as a 'front-man'. He got paid a nice amount of money to have his name on the clubs licensing plate. If the club or the book shop was raided, it was people like Jack who dealt with the police. It was designed to keep the Maltese owners out of trouble. She said Jack was a very clever man with businesses all over Soho and Scotland. Jack was in his forties and was married to one of Rene's sisters but they had been separated for years. He remained good friends with the rest of her family and they often all went out drinking together.

The shift finished and I arranged to meet Rene in the Red Lion later that evening. Then I went straight to the strip-club to see Jon to hand in my notice and to say thank you for the help he had given me but it was now time to move on.

He was pleased I had gone in to tell him and not just disappeared like others had before and said if I ever changed my mind and needed work to call back in and see him.

The Red Lion was really busy when I walked in. Rene was with a crowd of people I had not seen before and called me over. With her was a short, frumpy, black woman who looked in her late 30s. Not dressed for Soho I thought.

This was Dora, Rene's friend. Rene said that Dora was particular. Everything had to be kept clean and tidy. Dora laughed and said she wasn't that bad. She said if I wanted the room I could have a trial for a month. It would be £50 week cash. She added that she would prefer I didn't take people back to her home unless it was a boyfriend I was seeing. It was my turn to laugh; I hadn't got time to meet lads and didn't know enough people yet to invite them back. It was all sorted. I would move in the very next day. She lived in a place called The Borough near the Elephant and Castle.

Dora was an oddity - not the sort of person you would expect to find working in the sex industry of Soho. She was deeply religious with very strong beliefs. Her home was a little council property, exceptionally clean and everything was very ordered.

The room I had was clean with a double bed, a wardrobe and pictures of black children and black women carrying fruit baskets. The house was always warm and comfortable, much better than being cramped up in the hostel. Dora would cook the most amazing food, all afro-Caribbean. If I was lucky enough to be at home when she cooked, I'd have rice and peas with curried goat. I didn't eat meat at that time but had the sauce, which was superb.

Dora and I got on very well. We gave each other plenty of space as we usually worked opposite shifts. I was a lot younger than her and she mothered me. Her children were back in Jamaica and lived with her parents. All the time I knew her she sent a fair bit of money home each week.
She didn't drink or smoke and when she wasn't working she went to church. Her house was in a very rough area with a high crime rate. I usually caught a taxi back when I finished work as I didn't fancy walking back on my own from the tube station.

Work was going well and I got on with all the girls. They really looked out for me being a new girl. Rene had invited me to her little boy's second birthday. She said that I would meet her brother and the rest of her family there. We were quite excited about it.

Dougie gave Rene and me the morning off to go to Oxford Street and get something to wear for the party. We chose our outfits and had some lunch. After lunch we had a slow walk back to Maximillian's to do the evening shift.

After a few punters had gone in, a Scandinavian looking man came to the door. He seemed to have plenty of money and asked about the girls and what they looked like, then he went downstairs.

After a few minutes Maggie came upstairs laughing, saying

'That last punter you sent down! He only wants to buy you a cocktail!'
I panicked.

Maggie laughed and said

'Come on he's waiting!'

I asked her on the way down what I should say to him. She said I should just talk about what he wanted to talk about.

'Don't tell him anything truthful about yourself. Just make it all up.'

Dressed in jeans and tee-shirt I was probably the least sexy hostess in the West End, but he refused the company of anyone else. I went into the candlelit cubicle and sat down. He seemed friendly and I asked him why he had chosen me. He said I had a nice face. I felt very uncomfortable talking to him but chatted anyway. He said he was on business in London for two nights and that he travelled a lot with his work.

He offered to buy me another drink so I ordered one. Rene brought the drinks over and after a few more minutes brought the bill. I was pleased to see her as I was running out of conversation.

The bill was over £300 but he paid it straight away, without question. Rene then asked him for a booking fee as I was a special request. The booking fee was another £300. He paid this and asked if he could see the show. I explained I didn't perform so he asked if I would sit with him while he watched. I said that I didn't mind if that was what he wanted.

When the show finally started, I had to try hard to stop myself laughing. It was just Maggie lying on the bed performing sexy poses.

Then the showman suddenly appeared and, walking over to the bed asked Maggie if she liked big things.

'Oh yes!' she said.

He turned his back to us and pretended to unzip his trousers, looking over his shoulder and winking as if he was going to have the time of his life.
Maggie slid towards him on the end of the bed and said

'Oh God, it's huge!'

She bent her head down as if he was getting a blow-job.
After a couple of seconds he turned around and produced a big plastic banana.

It was all so tacky but the punter loved it, laughing and clapping at the ridiculous show. He said thank you and was still chuckling as he went back up the stairs. I waited a few minutes and then went back up to the door. The punter was still there and handed me his business card. He asked if I would like to go out for dinner with him as he had enjoyed my company. He had a laugh about the show, said it was definitely not what he had expected, then went on his way.

Rene popped upstairs and said I had done very well. And, as I had sat with him as a hostess, I could put my door money with theirs and split everything three ways, if I wanted to. This sounded good to me. She and Maggie always split everything down the middle, so if one had a bad shift and the other one made all the money it worked out quite well. When I got my money I had made £300! The best shift I'd had.

The day of the party I went home with Rene after work to get ready in her tidy flat near Stoke Newington. Her babysitter brought her little boy home. He was so pretty, with dark curly hair and long eyelashes that he could have passed for a little girl. And, so excited about his party.

People started to arrive. First was Wanda, then Dougie came home. Then Jack arrived with a young lad about the same age as I was, who was Rene's kid brother Danny. He was blonde and quite attractive with a broad Scottish accent. We spent some time chatting about how he had lived in Corby for quite a while but was thinking of moving up to London. Jobs were hard to find in the Midlands and he knew his sisters would find him a job in Soho.
Quite a few people had arrived by now and Jerry went to greet them. I didn't really know anyone at this time and the few I had met must have been working as I didn't recognise anyone. In those days I was quite shy, so I sat in a corner on my own. After a while Rene noticed me and whispered something to Wanda. Wanda came over and sat down on the floor next to me. Suddenly she reached over for a kiss. I panicked and moved away quickly. I felt like crying, beginning to wish I wasn't there. She moved closer again and put her hand on my leg. I jumped up, shouting that I wasn't into women and to fuck off and leave me alone.

The whole room erupted with laughter. Wanda winked at Rene; it had all been a wind-up to get me to wake up. Danny came to my rescue. The pair of them were always on a wind-up, he said. And, I had shown I could stick up for myself. Apparently that was well thought of in the Soho crowd. Rene came over and took my hand.

'Come and meet some of the gang,' she said.

I looked at her and we both started to laugh. I must admit that after that I felt far more at ease and went more with the flow of the party. I was talking to everyone, and didn't feel the odd one out anymore.

Some years after the party, Wanda was seeing a guy from the West End known for knocking women around. They fought all the time, usually when one or both of them were drunk. But, she would never leave him and this became so normal for them we got used to it.

One night we had all been in the Red Lion for a few drinks after work. Wanda said she would see us in the morning at the club. I gave her a hug then off she went. But, she didn't turn up for her shift which was really strange. None of us had mobiles in those days so we thought she had just had too many drinks and failed to get up for work. How wrong we were.

She had gone home and had the usual fight with the boyfriend, but it had gone too far this time and he had thrown her out of a window, three flights up and broken her back. We were told that she would never walk again and had to have a major operation.

The operation was successful; Wanda survived and did walk again but became even more dependent on drink. Her boyfriend was charged with attempted murder.

A few years later she came back to Soho and worked the odd shift. Wanda left Soho for good a short time before I did. She cut herself off completely from us all. None of us saw her again apart from Rene.
Happily, the last time I spoke to Rene, some years back, Wanda had met somebody, had a child and was very settled and very happy.

Danny had taken a bit of a shine to me and towards the end of the night asked if he could see me again. I had drunk quite a bit and giggling, asked how he could see me if he lived in Corby. But he had spoken to his sister and was staying for a while, working for Dougie in the club shop.

I said I would like to see him again but I wanted to take things very slowly. He agreed. I was ready to go home. It wasn't the best of areas where Rene lived so I accepted Danny's offer to come with me to get a taxi.

The next day I was on a late shift. I was a bit early and went downstairs to have a coffee with the girls. Rene was at the bar, reading. As soon as she saw me she jumped up and said,

'Well? How did you and my little brother get on last night then?'

I smiled and told her he had asked to see me again. She laughed to herself and said she knew we would hit it off. I asked her why, but she just grinned and said the boobs for one and you're blonde. I went red and she laughed.

The buzzer went and a punter came down the stairs. Rene sat him down. He ordered a beer and I poured it for her, using a glass that was already there from a previous customer, that had some beer left in it. This was a normal thing. If any beer was left in a glass they kept it and topped it up for the next punter. The beer was de-alcoholised and the cocktails were either orangeade or cherryade at a very expensive price.

When Rene got the beer, she moaned about the punter being an American and would be awful to get money out of. She asked him if he would like to buy her a drink, he agreed and she came back for a cocktail.

As she was on her own, she asked if I would bring the bill over for her. I must have looked worried but she said to just put the bill on the table and she would do the talking. There was a bill she had already used for a different punter, so I could use that. Then she sat back down with him. I left her to talk for a short time until she gave me the nod, then I took the bill over and placed it on the table, asking if he could settle the bill before the show started.

Sure enough, the American looked at the bill and yelled that he was being robbed. I panicked.

Rene got between me and the punter shouting in his face that he had been asked if he would like her company and he had said yes. It wasn't her fault that he had not read the prices first as there was a menu on every table and one on the door. (The price list on the door was slightly hidden)

Dougie heard the shouting and flew downstairs. He marched over and asked what the problem was. The punter looked at Dougie; well over 6 foot with a big beard, very well built with tattoo's everywhere. After seeing Dougie he thought better of it, and paid up straight away.

Dougie must have put the fear of God into the American. After he had paid, he waited for Dougie to move out of the way before running for his life upstairs and onto the busy street. The show was forgotten about in his rush to escape.

It was my first attempt at working the bar. Rene said I had done well. .

The bell went again and another punter arrived downstairs. He was strange looking, with a hat on with what looked like a dreadlock each side of his hat. He was dressed all in black and his trousers were too short for his legs. I giggled when I saw him - he looked so silly. Rene said that the man was an Hasidic Jew and asked if I had never seen anyone dressed like that before. I said that I hadn't. I didn't really know what an Hasidic Jew was; there weren't any where I came from. He sat down and ordered a Coke. Rene said these were worse than Americans to get money out of but the good thing was they wouldn't want to be seen to be coming in to a sex club. It would be very shameful for them. She also said they were nearly always loaded with money.

She asked if he would like to buy a drink for her. He said yes that he would.
Rene was dressed in fishnets with a sequined costume on, with her long blonde hair flowing, of course he was going to say yes to her. She called me over and asked if he would like to buy me a drink as well. He said yes, he would.

I went and sat down with Rene and the punter who I found to be a bit creepy. He looked like he had been to a funeral, but we sat and chatted to him. He was married with children and moved to England from Israel a number of years ago, setting up his own courier business.
Rene asked if he would like to buy us another cocktail and he readily agreed. He said that he liked blonde ladies very much, that he found them very sexy.
Soon enough, Dougie brought the bill over placing it on the table for the punter to pick up and pay.

The punter picked up the bill, got his wallet out, gave Dougie £5 and said grandly;

'You may keep the change'.

Rene and I looked at each other and I couldn't help a nervous giggle.
Dougie said to the punter that he hadn't read the bill correctly and to have another look.

He did that, then jumped up and threw himself on the floor wailing.

We all looked at each other. This was really odd. Rene told the punter to stop being stupid and get back on the chair to discuss the bill. He carried on wailing and making weird noises.
Then suddenly, he calmly got up and sat back down on the chair.
He said he couldn't possibly pay such a ridiculous amount of money.

Dougie was getting annoyed now and just wanted to get on with his work in the shop. He shouted at the man that he had chosen not one lady but two and chosen to buy us two cocktails each. The bill had to be covered.
The punter was trying so hard not to get his wallet out.
He said he had got plenty of money to pay the bill he just didn't want to.

'Fine, let's call the police in and take him to court.' Rene said.

The punter didn't like this idea very much and got his wallet out.
I had never seen so much money in my life. His wallet was full of £50 notes. His bill was £450 and as he handed the money over, I noticed Dougie drop one of the £50 notes on the floor and stand on it. I wasn't sure if I should tell him but before I got the chance he told the punter one of the notes was only a £5 note.
The punter looked a bit puzzled but Dougie showed him the notes and he didn't argue. He carried on paying and Dougie did the same again.

He said, 'You've given me that £5 again instead of a £50.'

The club lighting was dim with only red light bulbs and some candlelight, so he didn't argue, just paid up, and asked if he could leave. Like the previous punter, he ran back upstairs without seeing the show.

Dougie put the money behind the bar and was just about to go back upstairs when Rene called out to him.

'Oh not so fast Dougie!'

I looked at her and she winked at me and said,

'Well? What about the extra money that you switched? You know it goes three ways!'

Dougie laughed, put his hand in his pocket and handed me and Rene £30 each. He said he had got £40 for doing the switch. Rene told him he was cheeky but let it go. I was confused why he had given me the money and what the switch meant.

Rene then asked that if she got the doorman to stay on, would I like to work the rest of the shift downstairs as she was on her own. The doorman agreed to stay on, so I said I would. She suggested I go to Ann Summers to get something a bit sexier to work in. I nipped out and bought a lacy all in one and some fishnets and changed. I tied my hair up and when I came out Rene and Dougie both gave me a wolf-whistle.

'So you can look sexy then Maxine' they laughed.

I was so embarrassed.

This was my first hostess shift in Soho.

I would spend the next 12 years doing the job.

# Queen's Highway

Dougie, Rene's partner was a big man with a big heart. He was the archetypal gentle giant. He ran the video shop above Maximillian's and really looked after us. Any problems we had with punters he would run straight down the stairs and his appearance alone usually got the punters paying.

Although he couldn't read or write, Dougie was good with money and seemed to make it just by looking at it. He taught me how to do the switch, the little Maltese trick I had seen him do on the Jewish punter. The clubs were always quite dark with minimal lighting, often only lit by candlelight, so 'switching' was easy.

When settling a bill with a punter, you keep a folded £5 note in your hand. Then as the punter hands over twenty or fifty pound notes you surreptitiously drop one on the floor and hide it by standing on it, then you unfold the fiver and show them their 'mistake'. We made a lot of money that way, especially with the Japanese punters who always seemed to be carrying lots of £50 notes.

Dougie could smell money on punters. He had a knack of knowing, just by looking at them, if they were going to be worth our while. He would buzz down saying, 'this is a good one!' We knew then to try and get them to buy as many cocktails as possible while they sat with us.

Another of his little scams was what we called 'the booking fee'. The hostess would sit the punter down and get them drinks. When the bill was being paid, Dougie would look in the punter's wallet and, if he saw more money in there, the booking fee was added. After all, the punter had booked us to sit with him.

It was all quite easy really but it was never written on the pricelist as it was a completely made up, spontaneous extra charge. The booking fee could be anything from £20 to £300, depending on how much money they had left.
We didn't like them leaving with money unspent.

I've never known anyone since who could make as much money in as many ways as Dougie could.

Mario was one of Dougie's business partners. He was a tall, very good looking man who had been an athlete in Malta as a young man. He worked alongside Dougie in the shop part of the business selling pornographic videos and magazines. Mario, like Dougie; was always ready to help out if we had any problems downstairs. He was, however, a little less demanding with the punters than Dougie; more mindful that they could call the police at any time. If the club got into trouble it would affect the video shop too. And, vice versa, if the shop was raided it affected the hostess bar in the same building.

The shop was having problems at that time like similar shops in Soho. When there was a raid, the police would close us down and search for what seemed like forever, looking for illegal, banned porn.

The police were always plainclothes officers and usually the same ones would carry out every raid. We got to know some of them and would have a laugh when they asked if we had hidden the videos in the toilets or elsewhere. It was a game of cat and mouse. The lads upstairs always left a couple of videos for them to find but the rest were taken away just before the raid, unless ours was the first club on the list. As soon as one club in Soho was raided a quick call or a dash through the tunnels to the other shops warned them they could be next.

Mario was a very discreet man and kept his private life to himself. I think that I only met his wife once in the 10 years I worked with him. She was from Thailand and worked away a lot. They had no children when I knew him. Occasionally, he came out for a drink after work with us when we would go for a Chinese, then on to a disco or club.

Bop was a little guy. Again, he had a big heart. He was one of the funniest men that I have ever met, always joking with the girls and he would bring us cups of coffee and little treats. I never saw this little man in a bad mood. He also always used to run down helping us out with the difficult punters even though he was tiny, around 5 feet tall. He and the tall, handsome Mario were like a comedy act.

He was the third partner in the business. They were all the best of friends and ran a tight outfit. Nothing was ever a problem to them and they actually did seem to care about us girls, where most of the club owners didn't. Bop was also Maltese. As all the men did, he spoke about business in Maltese. They taught us how to swear in Maltese and some key words, for when the punters had money. We learned, 'haft na floose' which meant they had no money and 'mandish floose' which meant they had plenty. These three guys taught me a lot on how to survive Soho.

By this time, I had been seeing Danny regularly for a couple of months and we were always together. I still lived with Dora and worked at Maximillian's, mostly working on the door but doing a couple of shifts as a hostess. I worked most of my shifts with Rene and Maggie. I was happy with that as I got on very well with both of them.

One morning I went into work, went straight downstairs and Sadie was there on her own. I was supposed to be on the door that morning but Sadie said they wanted me downstairs working as a hostess. Rene was not very well and Mario had got the door covered. I didn't mind as it was quite a cold morning and I welcomed being downstairs in the warm.

Mario then came downstairs and asked if I could work a double shift. I had nothing planned so agreed to work with Sadie. I wasn't over-fond of her but the good money made it easier to tolerate her. We sat chatting for a while and she told me she had only worked in Soho for a little while. Her boyfriend was a Maltese guy who owned a different club.

She had just moved back to the UK after working as a stripper in Bahrain. I asked what it was like working in the Middle East but she didn't seem to want to say too much about it, just said the Arabs had loads of money but were a bit rough.

She asked me what I thought of Soho so far. I told her I was enjoying it, liked meeting the people and was amazed at how busy the place was. Then the buzzer went and the first punter came down the stairs. Sadie sat him down and ordered a coke and a cocktail. The gentleman was German. The buzzer went again and a group of Japanese men came down. Sadie grinned at me and nodded that this was good. They ordered some drinks and I asked if I could join them. They said I could so I sat on the table as I wasn't confident enough to sit on the chairs in the middle of the group. I asked if they would buy me a cocktail and they did.

Sadie wanted me to take her customer's bill over. I excused myself from the Japanese and walked over to the counter and turned the music up a little bit. It was an old trick I had been taught, to make sure other punters couldn't hear what was being said by any disgruntled customers.

We were lucky as the German paid straight away but stayed where he was, waiting for the show to start. I went back and sat with the Japanese group. Sadie came over and asked if she could join us for a cocktail. One of them agreed so we both sat talking to them, with the drinks flowing.

Before we knew it, we had drunk five cocktails each. It was the most I'd ever had bought for me. Sadie excused herself to work out the bill and call Mario downstairs to present it to the unsuspecting tourists. When Mario came over with the bill, the Japanese argued about the cost, getting quite loud.

The German man came over. We were expecting him to take their side but he said he had paid his bill so they must pay theirs. They seemed to listen to him and paid their bill, in Stirling and Yen. They were loaded so it was a real shame that the German man was still in the club. They had so much money left we could easily have charged them a large booking fee. But, as the German hadn't paid one we couldn't suddenly charge them. The show was performed by Sadie, it was the same poor sort of show I had seen previously, but the Japanese and the German finished their drinks and seemed quite happy when they left.

Later, Dougie came downstairs to take over from Mario. He asked if we had been busy and we told him about the Japanese punters. Of course he came up with more ways that we could have handled it and got more money. He said we should've asked the German if he would like to call back later for the show and that we should've given him a pass for free drinks to get him out of the way. Failing that we could also have turned the music up much higher and put our backs to the other punter so it would be difficult for them to see or hear anything. Either way would have got us a large booking fee from the Japanese.

The buzzer went again and another customer came down the stairs. Sadie served him the Coke he asked for. He must've suddenly realised that the club was not the place for him as he asked to pay straight away. Sadie tried to tell him that there was an automatic hostess fee with any drink which was purchased. As she did so the punter threw the money for the drink at her and then jumped the length of the table. Knocking Sadie out of the way, he bolted up the stairs as fast as he could go. My guess is he had been done before in a similar club to ours. I checked that Sadie was alright. She just shrugged and said it was all in a days work.

As the shift wore on I began to notice Sadie flirting with Dougie. They were playing cards and asked if I wanted to join them in a game of Calookie, a Maltese game. I wasn't into card games and declined. They seemed to be sitting very close to each other with Sadie occasionally resting her hand on Dougie's leg. I asked if they minded me going out for a coffee and a newspaper. Neither of them did, but they told me not to be too long as it was my turn to meet and greet. Sadie added that if a customer did come in she would sit with them until I returned.

I went to the coffee shop, bought a paper and went straight back. It was unusually quiet on the streets and I ran downstairs to tell Sadie that I thought it would be a quiet shift. When I got down there I couldn't see or hear Sadie or Dougie, which I thought was very strange. After checking behind the bar I thought to look in the changing room. When I tried to open the door I found Dougie had his back to it and Sadie was crouched in front of him giving him a blow-job. I was shocked, and, she had seen me.

I went back and sat down behind the bar. They both appeared a while later looking a bit embarrassed. Dougie spoke first and asked if I could forget what I had just seen. I just nodded in reply.

I wondered how Sadie could work alongside Rene when she was doing her partner at the same time and, I was shocked at Dougie as well. He was the last person I thought would mess around.

I felt quite uncomfortable for the rest of the shift. Sadie and I didn't really have much to say to each other. Dougie went back upstairs and didn't come back down again during my shift. I was glad when it finished and went straight home.

My next shift was the following morning, a double-shift with Rene. After what I had seen the day before in the changing room, I really wasn't looking forward to it. On my way to work I picked up the morning coffees and a newspaper.
Dougie was just opening up when I arrived and he didn't look very happy.
I went downstairs, said hello to Rene and gave her a coffee. She just grunted at me, she didn't seem to be in a good mood either; definitely not her usual bubbly self.

I didn't push it. I just sat down and had my drink while I flicked through the newspaper. After a while, Rene told me she and Dougie had fallen out the night before. They'd had a big argument as she was convinced he was seeing someone else. She looked straight at me as she said this, like she was accusing me. I don't know what she saw in my face but she suddenly jumped off her seat and grabbed hold of my hair, gripping it in her fist and while she punched and kicked me. I tried to defend myself as best I could but she had the element of surprise and got the better of me.

Dougie and Bop ran downstairs to see what was going on. When Dougie got to the bottom of the stairs and saw Rene attacking me he threw himself at us shouting in Maltese. Apparently he was telling her that it wasn't me he was seeing. Finally, Rene let go of my hair. She turned and looked at him as if to say, 'if it's not her, then who is it?' Dougie just shook his head and went back up the stairs.

I was so angry. Not only had I seen it all the day before and been put in an awkward position, but now I'd had a slap for something I hadn't done. We still had most of the shift left to get through with Rene very quiet and me still very angry.

It was a relief when the buzzer went and a punter came down the stairs. I went over and introduced myself, sat the punter down, asked if I could join him and would he like a drink. He said he would so I grabbed a cocktail.

While I was sitting with him, I worried that Rene might have said something to Danny about me messing around with her man. That would, no doubt, be the end of our relationship.

Danny was supposed to be meeting me after the shift finished. The punter ordered another cocktail and Rene brought the bill over. The punter hadn't quite got enough money to settle it so she took the money he had towards the bill and his details. While he went off to the bank and we walked back to the bar, Rene suddenly put her hand on my shoulder and said she was very sorry, she really had thought it had been me who was seeing Dougie. She said with me being blonde, younger and prettier, she had thought it must have been me. I was just how Dougie liked them. She added that she thought it had been going on for some time.

I said she should think about who else worked alongside her but I refused to give a name. I hoped she would work it all out for herself, given time. She then asked if she could take me out for a drink after work to apologise. I told her I was meeting her brother then, but that she was welcome to join us. We were only going out for a drink locally anyway. The rest of the shift went smoothly. We always worked well together and were soon chatting as usual; as though the morning's events had never happened.

Just as we were clearing up to finish our shift, the buzzer went. I went to greet the punter but laughed when I realised it was Danny. Rene shouted over,

'Are you buying her a cocktail then bro?'

'Not a chance at these prices! All you get is a glass of cherryade!' he said, winking at me.

As Rene was walking off after locking up, she told Dougie that she was going out for a drink with Danny and me; he didn't have a chance to respond.

We went to The Intrepid Fox on Wardour Street. As usual the music was loud. Jerry and Rene went over to the bar and I went for a wander, going up a big staircase that led to an upstairs bar. I had been in the pub before, but never in this bar. The wall coverings were plastered wall to ceiling with posters advertising gigs and different bands.

I thought it was amazing.

The upstairs bar was quite small with a tiny bar in the shape of the front of a car and the stools were old engines.

It all looked very gothic, with chandeliers and coat-hooks which were a pair of metal hands sticking out of the wall. It was a strange but cool place to be seen in at the time.

Rene and Danny found me upstairs. I was still looking around open mouthed at the place. Then Maggie walked in with her big brother Don and two other men, Big Ade and Little Ade. I remember thinking Big Ade was scary looking. He had his head shaved with a floppy bit of hair left long at the front. He had just two teeth at the front of his mouth, the rest of them, he said, had been lost in many battles in the West End and north of the border. He was from Glasgow and mad as a hatter. He was a despatch rider who also sold drugs out of the courier top box on his motorbike. He was a very funny man.

When he found out that his girlfriend was pregnant, he disappeared from the West End, reappearing after a short while to announce that he and his partner now had a little boy.

We asked him where he had been. He said,

'I have a car outside, come with me and I'll show you'

We jumped into his car and he took us to his house. We met his girlfriend and their lovely baby boy and he showed us his garden. There was a wall on which he had painted hills and birds and a loch, complete with boat. We were all stoned and just stood there staring at the mural for ages. It was fantastic and we told him so. He gave us a toothless grin and said that he had done it so his boy would think he was growing up in Scotland.

A short while after this Ade was riding through the West End. A taxi braked suddenly and he skidded to avoid it. The top box flew open and wraps of speed, weed and sheets of LSD flew out onto the road.

Unfortunately for him, two policemen in a car saw it happen. Ade tried to pick everything up but it was too late. He was caught red-handed and received five years in prison.

We tried to stay in contact with him but he didn't want anything to do with anyone from the West End after that. I saw Ade, maybe twice after he got out of prison. He was never the same again.

He disappeared, like so many others I knew over the years in Soho.

Little Ade was a short, bubbly man with a broad Manchester accent, a little man with a huge heart who would help out anyone in trouble. But, you would only cross him once. If you did, he changed instantly from gentle little guy from Manchester into a well connected, half-Maltese gangster who took no crap from anyone. He was the boss at a nightclub in Soho.

He seemed at odds with the scene and crowd he mixed with. He dressed differently and often looked out of place, but he seemed popular with everyone. We had loads of fun with Little Ade over the years. We went to festivals, parties, out for meals and clubbing together in our little group. I always felt fortunate simply having him as a friend. Ade was a fun guy to be around in those days. Later, he had a fiery relationship with a woman called Scatty Annie. Both had very short fuses but they lasted a good while before they ended up physically fighting on numerous occasions.

I took an instant liking to both of the Ade's. It was a good night, that night in The Fox. When Danny and I got back to Dora's, we could hear people talking in the house. Danny recognised the voice as Jack's, Rene's ex-brother in law. I wondered what he would be doing there with Dora.

Dora was busy cooking Jack a meal. I thought they were a strange combination but if it made her happy then it was her choice. She invited us to eat with them which pleased Danny who had been moaning about being hungry all the way home. The meal looked lovely. Jack obviously thought his luck was in and was quite charming. After a while Danny and I excused ourselves and went up to bed. We didn't hear the front door go, so we guessed that Jack was staying the night.

In the morning, we found Jack snoring away on the sofa. He woke up when we walked in and sat up. We asked how he had got on. Nothing had gone on, he scowled. Dora had demanded an AIDS test and said she didn't believe in sex before marriage.

I went in to work, on the door. Danny turned up later and said he had some bad news. He had to go back to Corby for a while, he had family problems and had other things to sort out as well, but he didn't say what they were. Then he was gone. I was upset but I carried on working. Maggie was working downstairs. I must have looked miserable when she came up to get coffees as she stopped to see if I was alright.

I told her about Danny. She dismissed it and told me to forget him. I was to come out with her and her friends that night to The Fox. We got ready at work when the shift finished and went straight there. It was as busy as usual. We found her brother Don in the bar cracking jokes. He was such a funny guy.

We were playing pool when a man walked over to us. He was so odd looking, wearing a kilt accompanied by Doc Martens and a ripped t-shirt. He had the wildest hair I had ever seen. It was a mass of black hair wrapped up into a ball on the top of his head with chopsticks pushed through the middle.

Maggie hugged him and introduced him as Adam. Later on, both of the Ade's appeared. It was a good crowd. We all sat around talking. The men were arguing about religion. They were all from Scotland but had different religions. We were laughing at their heated debate. It was quite amusing to hear best mates going on at each other like that over religion.

After a while, another man with long red hair and who looked like a biker appeared, wearing a bandana. Adam introduced me to him. His name was Don from Northern Ireland. He was as mad as the others but refused to get into the big debate about religion. Don and 'Scottish Don' (Maggie's brother) used to have long discussions about everything and anything. I didn't know it then but Don would become my husband a few years later.

He was a real West End character but involved in the music side of things rather than the seedy aspects of Soho. Don never worked in any of the clip joints. He was the resident DJ at The Marquee. This meant we had some good, free nights, watching the live bands that played there. Then of course there was the 'Green Room', where the bands would hold their own little parties following the gigs. . .

I remember Scotty Don was doing a bit of dealing at one time in north London. He asked Don to go with him. A man who called himself 'Spider' owed him a lot of money. This guy never seemed to want to pay up what he owed. Don went with him and they knocked on the door of Spider's flat. Spider's girlfriend, who was called 'Moonbeam', answered the door. She was completely off her face. She let them in and as they walked in, Spider was injecting speed into his groin. The two Don's stood there watching him. When he had finished he told them he had no money.

Scotty Don was not a happy bunny and gave Spider a bit of a seeing to which seemed to jog his memory and he managed to find the money he hadn't got a few minutes earlier.

Scotty asked Don what late payment penalty he thought Spider should pay for the five minute delay. Don saw a big pile of weed on a table and even more speed. He told Scotty he thought that would suffice. For quite a few minutes, Spider begged them to only take the weed and leave him the speed. They told him to shut the fuck up, and helped themselves.

The two Don's left Spider's place quite happy, having not only recovered the money owed but also got the drugs as a bonus. That was how things worked in London and most major cities in those days. I think things would have been handled far more brutally now.

Some time after Don and I had got together, I remember Little Ade buying a new motorbike. It was a Kawasaki replica Harley. It was the easy rider style and a very smart bike. After he had bought it, he came round to our flat to show Don and I asked him if I could take it for a spin. Ade being Ade just laughed and threw me the keys, so off I went. I took it onto the A406 up near Wembley and remembering friends who lived there, thought I'd call round to see them.

They had just lit a joint as I arrived, so I joined them. It was three hours later before it occurred to me that perhaps, I should get back. After my smoke a three hour absence didn't seem to be at all unreasonable.

As I rode back up the hill, I saw Ade at the top of a lamp post looking quite frantic and Don was doing what looked like a war dance. I pulled up, wondering what the hell was going on. They both started shouting at me, 'where had I been?' They thought I had been knocked off the bike,

Being stoned, I just thought they were a bit manic and found it all quite funny, much to their annoyance, but after a joint themselves they saw the funny side of it, especially when I reminded Ade he had climbed a lamppost to find me.

On the night I met Adam and Don in the Fox and had such a good time, they all decided they would go back to Little Ade's for a smoke and invited me along. We left The Fox following last orders and we walked through Soho to Little Ade's flat. On the way Big Ade was laughing.

'I must warn you, Ade's decorating is a bit dodgy!' he said.

We arrived at his flat which was above a club. We went through a small doorway and up a load of stairs. He opened the door and the whole flat was pink. I started laughing, thinking about what Big Ade had said. They all explained that Little Ade was colour blind and the only colour that was distinct to him was pink. It was a really funky flat, Ade's bed was suspended from the ceiling and a big, glass fronted tank went from the ceiling to the floor and ran the whole width of the room. It housed a 15 foot Boa Constrictor called 'Cool'.

Everyone grabbed one of the bean-bags scattered around and Ade brought out a large glass table from behind the sofa.

He put some music on. I felt happy and content with this crowd and very relaxed. Maggie was sat next to me. We got on so well, she was telling me that she had a long-term boyfriend in prison for drug-dealing.

That should have been a sign, a warning but it didn't register at the time.

Just as we were all relaxing, Little Ade suddenly said,

'Right, I've got a job to do before we get too wasted. Do I have any helpers, apart from Adam?'

They all laughed at this but I didn't have a clue what he was going on about. He got up and took a picture from his wall and delved into the safe concealed behind it. He produced a huge bag of white powder. I looked at Maggie and she winked at me.

'Looks like it's going to be a good night,' she giggled.

I was still wondering what was going on and what she meant but didn't let on I didn't know. Ade tipped the bag onto the table and found a set of scales. He weighed the powder out and put it into little bags. Adam and Don assisted him with this and it was all done in no time at all. Then, he fetched a burner and set of test tubes.

The atmosphere was charged as Ade put some powder into the test tube. He heated it up until it formed a little lump and then put the lump into a funny looking pipe and lit it.

This was crack. Well before its time. It was the 80's and this drug wasn't really recognised until years later.

We all had a go. I felt like I needed to rush off and do loads of things but I didn't actually move. Ade made little lines of the white powder on the table and they all took turns snorting it.

Ade asked if I had ever done coke before and when I said no, told me to lick my finger and rub some into my gums first.
The hit from the pipe had soon faded so I did what he said with the coke. My whole mouth became numb, it was such a weird feeling but I did like it. I decided then I was ready to try a line. I snorted it. As it dropped down my throat it felt disgusting and I threw up straight away, with them all laughing at me.

I felt fine once I had been sick.

Big Ade rolled a joint and passed it round. My head was spinning; I was definitely away with the fairies at that point. Everyone seemed to be talking at the same time but I couldn't seem to get any words to come out. I can't remember how long I was like that for, but people seemed to drift off without me noticing. In the end there was just me, Maggie and Ade. Ade said we could stay over and pulled the bed out the bottom of the sofa and we slept on that.

The next morning I was a little worse for wear. Everything seemed very slow. I was glad when I got to work that I was downstairs. Maggie wasn't working but she popped by to see if I had enjoyed the night and to say she was going to go to The Fox again that night if I wanted to come. I said I was going home first to let Dora know I was alright. Then I would get showered and meet them later. Over the next few years Maggie and I would become inseparable.

Work was good that day and we had some great punters in. Towards the end of the night we had an older English gentleman come in. He was wearing a suit and looked like he worked in the City. He bought me three cocktails and was charming. Just before the bill was brought over he asked if I would do the show for him. I told him I was pretty new and didn't do shows yet. He laughed and asked if I was shy. He said that as I didn't do the shows would I perform a private strip for him? I said I would have to ask the girl at the bar. Rene grinned when I told her,

'Little Miss Innocent won't be innocent anymore, now she's started stripping!'

She grabbed my arm and said to watch her. She danced around and went topless. I said I would do it if he paid the full bill. He paid the bill and £200 on top for his private strip.

Rene showed him to the back room and put a small stereo on playing Marvin Gaye's Sexual Healing. I started to gyrate to the music remembering the girls in the strip bar I had seen when I worked in Kings Cross. I danced right up to him then turned my back round and took my top off. Just as the record finished I faced him criss-crossing my hands over my boobs. That was it. Show over. The punter was happy with the show and I was happy with the show money.

Rene asked how it had gone. To be honest, it meant nothing to me; I seemed able to take it in my stride.

Maggie came down just before the end of the shift and said Dora was working at Erotica. I went to see her there to show her I was alright and went to Maggie's to get ready. On the way, Maggie said she had to meet Ade as he might have a flat above the same club as his that had become empty and which she wanted to rent. She asked if I would like to go with her. I didn't mind so we went to see him and she asked him about it. He said the rent was so high it would need two to share. She looked at me and I considered it.

Yes, Dora was nice, but living with her involved a lot of travelling. My social life in Soho was improving. This flat was in the middle of Soho underneath Ade's. I knew Maggie and I would always get on, so I made my mind up to move in with her. I told Dora and she was fine about it as long as I paid the next month's rent so she had time to find someone else to rent my room. I paid that in cash there and then and we moved in the following day.

The flat was cosy and furnished. Which was lucky as Maggie and I mostly had just clothes and shoes to move in with. We had a flat warming party the first night, rushing round inviting people, telling them to bring what they wanted in the way of booze. The party started and about twenty people turned up. It was a small flat so that was more enough. Ade opened his flat up as well and people drifted between the two.

Maggie took some acid and persuaded me to try it with her. I didn't know what it was supposed to do. I didn't know anything about it but thought, why not? After all it was a party.

We were up in Ade's flat at the time, sitting on one of his big pink sofas, Maggie, Ade and me. On the back of one sofa he had an old ladies fox-fur scarf. It had three foxes heads on the end. I didn't like fur or dead animals and it made me feel sick at the best of times.

I took the acid and nothing seemed to happen for ages. Maggie said it was the same for her although she kept laughing randomly. When I asked what she was laughing at she didn't know. I sat watching Pink Floyd's The Wall video, Ade's favourite.

As I was sat there in a world of my own, I could see something moving out of the corner of my eye. I looked round, Maggie had gone but Ade was still in the room. It must have been him.

A few moments later, I saw something move again, out of the corner of my eye. I looked round quickly. Nobody there, except, the fox-fur, which was looking at me, angrily.

I looked at Ade to see if he could see them too but he was watching his film, stoned.

I could still feel the malevolent gaze and, fearfully, looked across again. The fox-fur was still looking straight at me. I was horrified and froze.

I wasn't aware that acid was a mind-altering drug; no-one had bothered to tell me. Ade was away with the fairies and the fox-fur was still staring at me. I was absolutely petrified.

I tried to ignore it but, as scared as I was, I couldn't help myself and had to keep looking over at it, terrifying myself even more with every furtive glance. Every time I did, it looked more and more evil until finally, with rabid foam spilling out of all three mouths, it snarled savagely at me. I screamed as loudly as I could. Ade nearly fell off the chair he was sitting on.

'Shit Max, what's wrong?' he said.

I yelled at him to get out of the room before the fox got him and he laughed his head off which made my panic even worse.

The fox-fur was getting angrier and I was getting more and more terrified. I felt as though I was going insane with fear but at the same time, I had a mission. I had to get rid of the fox-fur before it got both of us.
Ade beat me to it. At last, he got up out of his chair and grabbed it. He wrestled it as he opened the safe, then managed to slam the door on it. It was gone. I was so relieved. But, I could still hear it spitting and snarling from inside the locked safe.

My screams had attracted the attention of the other guests, some of whom came up to see what the fuss was all about. Ade told everyone about what he was calling my 'bad trip' and they were all laughing. Someone told me about good and bad trips and what had happened to me.

I decided there and then that acid was not the drug for me. I tried smoking a bit of weed and managed to calm down, but the experience had shaken me. Maggie too, laughed her head off when someone told her about it.

The horrible feeling stayed with me until the next day and I got to work a little later than usual. I was working on the door. For once I was pleased when it was very quiet to start with, but it got busier as the morning progressed.

'Live show! Sexy girls! Come inside for £2! Sexy girls, real live shows!'

I was still calling out as I reached down to put the heater on. When I came back up, there was a policeman with a grey beard standing at the door.

'Why are you calling out?' he asked.

'You know it is against the law and if I hear you again I will arrest you,' he said.

He walked away and I left it for a few minutes then called out again and magically, the same policeman bounced back in front of me. He had been hiding a couple of doorways up.

'You're nicked for obstruction of the Queen's highway,' he said as he grabbed me.

A police van arrived just as I called out to Mario who was working in the shop. It took me to the police station - West End Central - with a very smug looking policeman in tow.

West End Central was very busy when we arrived. They threw me into a cell while they sorted out the paperwork; or so they told me. I was held in the cell for over an hour and then all I got was a warning. They told me not to work any club doors again. If I did I would risk being arrested again.

After the warning I was free to go and went straight back to the club and on the door. Mario asked what had happened and said I was lucky to have got away with just a warning. I resumed calling out to possible punters again and luckily this time, no police appeared.

I needed a quiet night that evening. The last seven days had seemed like one big party. Maggie said she felt the same so she met me when I finished work and we picked a video up on the way home. Maggie was a bit on edge as we entered. There was a strange looking man sitting on our sofa. I looked at Maggie and, obviously feeling very awkward, she said,

'Max, meet Jerry'.

This was the boyfriend that she had mentioned before. I was puzzled,

'I thought he was in prison?'

She looked very guilty and admitted he was on the run.

'Can he stay here for a while?' she asked.

I looked at her in amazement thinking she must be joking. She wasn't.

Jerry spoke in an Irish accent, telling me he was sorry he had arrived without notice but he couldn't cope with prison anymore and had escaped with help from a friend. He had a drug problem and needed Maggie and me to help him, just for a couple of days. He added he would be moving on to his grandmother's house after.

He obviously didn't intend going anywhere so I was more or less forced to agree. I don't think it would've mattered what we said, he would've just stayed anyway.

I must admit I was terrified of this man. He was tall and skinny with weird scars on his face. He was sweating profusely and looked so unpleasant. What the hell did Maggie see in him? I wondered.

He told Maggie that she would have to go and score some heroin for him. I didn't know what 'scoring' meant. Maggie just nodded at him and left the flat. I was left there with the horrible stinking Jerry. The half hour I spent alone with him was the most uncomfortable thirty minutes of my life.

He didn't speak, just sat staring at the door waiting for her to return, which seemed to be taking forever. Eventually, very stressed, she returned, glancing at me apologetically as she handed him some paper containing heroin. He got straight up out of the chair and asked for some silver foil for his gear. I still didn't have a clue what was going on.

Maggie got a Kit-Kat out of her bag. She took the chocolate out of the wrapper and gave him the foil. He opened the little bit of paper Maggie had given him and put a bit of heroin on the foil. He lit a lighter under it to burn the drug. As the heroin burnt it produced smoke which he inhaled through a rolled up bank note. He chased the powder round and round the foil until it had all been burned. The sweet, sugary smell made me feel sick, but he looked more relaxed now and smiled.

A knock came on the door. Jerry jumped up and hid, telling us not to let anyone in. It was Ade; he only wanted to know if we were going out that night. Before I could answer Maggie said quickly that we didn't want to go out and that we were having a quiet night in for a change. Ade left and Jerry came out of hiding. He asked Maggie to sit down with him, which she did. I left the room for a few minutes and when I came back in Maggie had the foil and was joining him in inhaling what was on there.

Jerry asked if I would like to try some. In those days I would try anything once so

'Why not?' I said.

Maggie warned that it would be better if I didn't as it was very addictive, but Jerry had other ideas; he had already got some out onto the foil and was preparing the brown powder for me to inhale. It would relax me, he said. I chased the brown stuff round the foil with the lighter underneath.

Then I sat back, and was sick everywhere.

'It's your first time.' Maggie said.

'It always does that to people the first time they take it.'

When the sickness passed, I felt numb and couldn't move, a bit like the Pink Floyd song 'Comfortably numb'.

The feeling of warmth and well-being was amazing. I knew I would like this drug.

We carried on smoking every now and again that night and I even began to take to Jerry. He told me how bad prison had been for him and begged us not to tell anyone that he was around, especially not any of the Maltese. He had ripped a good few of them off over the years. Add that to his drug habit and you could understand why he wasn't the most popular person in Soho.

The next morning, as I got up to go to work, Maggie asked if I could say she was sick as she wanted some time with Jerry. Of course, I did.

We were really busy. It was getting close to Christmas and the place was electric with excitement. Rene was working the bar. We had a few groups of lads in. They were usually a nightmare as they wanted everything but didn't want to pay anything. I sat down with a group of English businessmen who tried to grope me whenever they could. I was dressed in black bra, knickers and stockings and they were all trying to have a free feel. It was quite unpleasant. I was struggling to control them, so Rene came over.

One of the group just laughed when the bill was given to him and then he shoved me so hard I went flying across the floor. Rene jumped on him and it turned into a bit of a brawl. Dougie came bounding down the stairs.

They took one look at Dougie and all charged towards him, knocking Rene and me flying again. Deftly, Dougie side-stepped and they all fell up the stairs, scrambling to the top. When they got upstairs they threw a chair and the little heater down to the bottom. Rene told me I should get used to it.

'It's always the same at Christmas-time. Lads out on the piss, think they can come in and do what ever they like.'

Shortly after the fracas, Little Ade came in and asked if I would like to go out with the gang that night. They would all be in The Fox around 10 o'clock, then they planned going on to a club. I said I might as well join them. He then added that it might be a good idea if I wore PVC or leather. I looked at him and he laughed.

'The club we are going to tonight is a bit different!'

And with that he was gone.

After work I walked up to the Zeitgeist leather and PVC shop. Money wasn't a problem then, I always had loads. It was a strange shop with things in it I didn't know what you would do with like chains and whips. There was a big vault door with handcuffs and leg-cuffs attached to it.

I thought the shop was amazing and being quite into uniforms at the time, I bought one that I thought would be good to work in. Then I went downstairs to 'the chamber' as it was known and chose a rubber top with pointed nipples and a pair of tight black rubber trousers. I finished off the outfit with thigh-high PVC boots. The man behind the counter asked if I worked in the clubs. I replied that I did so he gave me a discount and advised me to put talc on the rubber before I put it on to make it easier to slide into the rubber outfits.

Rene was still working when I went back to the club to pick my things up. It was quiet, apart from one man sat waiting for a show. She asked what I had bought, I showed her and she grinned.

'You've fitted in well with the Soho lifestyle Max,' she said

'Very different from the Little Miss Innocent who first arrived.'

I laughed, but it was true. I loved Soho and Soho seemed to like me. I went back to the flat where Maggie and Jerry were watching a video. I told them I was going back out but they were both out of it and probably didn't even realise I was there.

When I got to The Fox it was busy and the usual people were in there. I got a whistle from Little Ade. We played some pool and sat chatting until everyone had arrived. Irish Don came and I sat talking to him for ages about his life in Northern Ireland. When everyone else eventually arrived we headed off to a club called Gossips which was holding a fetish night.

It was all very weird. There were men crawling around on the floor wearing dog leads and being kicked every now and again by the other people in the club. They were slaves, someone told me. Other people were tied up and being whipped. The music was loud, gothic and heavy. I couldn't take it all in.

As I stood watching, a big woman with loads of hair asked if I would like to participate. She said she liked the look of me and would like to 'get into me'. I nearly died with shock. A woman was chatting me up!
Ade came to my rescue and told her I was with him. She floated off, kicking one of the slaves as she did so.

I liked some kinkiness but this was all too extreme. However, the music was good and we had a good time dancing to it. The atmosphere was electric. The big woman who had come over earlier seemed to be everywhere, never taking her eyes of me, which I found bizarre. The guys just found it funny. They kept saying that I had pulled and that she wanted to tie me up in her dungeon and, could they watch. Some of the group participated in a bit of bondage and I asked to be tied up too as I hadn't experienced it before. I found it exciting but I wasn't sure if I was more turned on by being tied or if I tied someone else up. It was buzzing in there. Little Ade had brought some cocaine with him and we all did the odd line in the toilets.

I noticed a door near the toilets which people were going in and out of. They all seemed to come out with cuts or blood on them. I asked Little Ade what was going on in there. He laughed and said it was the scratch and sniff room. I looked at him still none the wiser. He said people went in and a dominatrix woman would scratch their skin until blood came out. Then she would sniff the blood. He said I should go in and have a look for myself, so I did.

There were men and women getting cut and scratched by this weird woman. She was sniffing the blood as it pumped out. I got out of there pretty quickly. One of our group, Big Ade, had been in and he had a big gash in his arm. When I commented on it and said I had been in to have a look, he just grinned.

Around the main room, there were cages with various things inside them. There was the 'nipple clamp cage' or 'penis cage' where people were hung up and clamps were put on various parts of their body. It just looked a bit too much like pain with very little pleasure involved to me but I was definitely into whips so I had a go in the whip cage.

A woman dressed in a crotch-less black rubber all in one which showed her nipples was doing the whipping. I found that quite a turn on. Something else I liked was hot candle wax being poured over parts of the body. I was tied up at the time and it felt sensual and very sexy.

We all had a go at the different things. Little Ade and Adam seemed to be the most adventurous of our group. As the club got busier, Ade asked if anyone would like to go back to his place. It was early hours of the morning and we had been there quite a long time. We all said we would and we went back laughing at some of the mad things we had seen. It was certainly a night I would never forget.

The next day I was working a double shift with Rene. She asked how we had all got on and said she didn't like bondage but Wanda was well into it. That didn't surprise me after knowing about her 'Daddy' and, I'd seen Wanda being whipped the night before.

There was a new showman starting that day. He was from East London and was called Little Nicky. He had a great sense of humour and we hit it off straight away. We had some good punters in paying big bills. Rene had twisted her ankle and asked if I would do the show. I didn't mind as it was more like a comedy act really. We had a group of Dutch men in and the show was about to start. I noticed and wondered why Dougie and Mario had come down to see my show. I was posing on the bed touching my breasts and rubbing my crotch. Nicky came over and asked, loudly, if I would like to play with him instead, I said I would love to and he slid onto the bed. He was kissing my neck then he got off the bed, pulled down his trousers and actually got his dick out. Dougie and Mario were in stitches. It was Nicky's first show and also my debut and he actually thought he was getting the real thing. Not a chance!
I shot off the bed and said, '

'Thank you! Show finished, please call again!'

The punters looked puzzled but still left. Rene was laughing her head off. Suddenly her twisted foot didn't seem to bother her anymore. Someone told Nicky that he didn't have to get his dick out for real and we realised it had all been a set up and started laughing. Nicky said he was gutted he hadn't even got a blow-job out of it. The punters had paid over £600 just to see that excuse of a show. It was mad really when they could have had full sex from one of the girls who worked out of the nearby flats for a lot less.

Then we had a very odd punter come in who Rene had seen before; a regular at Erotica. She grinned when she saw him walk in.

'This one likes to argue about his bill but he always pays eventually. If you back down its game over and you won't get a penny. Be strong though and he will pay.'

I thought it all a bit strange but served him anyway. He was very odd. He didn't seem to want to do much talking and kept looking down at my legs and feet which made me feel awkward.

When Rene came over with the bill, she walked up to him and yelled straight in his face that he was a worthless piece of shit and he had better pay up. I had never heard Rene talking like that before, especially to a punter, but he seemed to enjoy it. The nastier she was, the more he liked it. He started to pay but stopped half-way through, looked at me and bent down and kissed my feet.

I burst out laughing but Rene stared at me to be quiet. He just smiled at me and finished paying the bill. I sat back down with him and he asked for my stiletto shoe. I passed one up to him and he started licking the heel. Then he licked inside the shoe. It was a strange experience to say the least.

Rene came over and said she would have to charge him more if he wanted to touch my feet. It was almost a whisper but he produced another £50 out of his wallet. I was a bit concerned as to what he was going to do but Rene just winked and said it was okay.

'It only takes a second,' she assured me.

He knelt on the floor in front of me and tickled my toes, then jumped up suddenly and ran to the toilet. After a while he came back out and then he just left.

I went back to the bar and Rene explained that he had a foot fetish.

'He's harmless enough, she said.

'He's been coming round the clubs for years. Sometimes he brings in a new pair of shoes and gets the girls to wear them.'

'At a price of course,' she quickly added.

I decided that the whole Soho thing was insane. I still couldn't get my head round some of it and I had been working there for a couple of years by this point. It was weird but fun at the same time with the nutty things that went on. I loved everything about it and enjoyed every minute of it.

Jerry was gone. He had been out trying to buy his 'brown' and been caught. We were very lucky we hadn't been found out hiding him and that Jerry didn't mention that he had been staying with us. He told the police he had been living rough.

Our drug taking spiralled once Jerry had gone. We were smoking heroin most days. Dougie once asked me if I was taking anything but of course I denied it. Smackheads were not wanted in the clubs. The Maltese didn't trust them due to them always needing more and more money to support their habit. If they weren't making enough money by normal means, then the punters bills had been known to disappear.

It was a Saturday morning and I walked in for my morning shift and got the surprise of my life. My father was sat at a table with Dougie! In a state of shock I gave him a hug, wondering what he was doing there. He told me he had come to take me home with him. Meanwhile, Dougie quickly disappeared, leaving us to it.

Unknown to me Rene and Dougie were worried. So worried that she had gone into my bag during one shift and found my parents phone number, given it to Dougie and he had rung them. He asked my father to come and take me home before I got too involved in the drug scene. They were concerned that I wouldn't be able to get off heroin. Meanwhile, I had carried on working hard and playing even harder.

I took my father for a coffee and told him that I was happy, that I was earning well and there was no chance I would be going home with him. Of course, he got emotional; after all I was still his little girl. He asked me outright if I took drugs. I denied it and said Dougie had just got it wrong, that he was just looking out for me. We had some lunch and reluctantly my father went back home alone. But, I had to promise that I would go home for a weekend sometime soon. He also made me promise to ring him at least twice a week. I went back to the club. Dougie seemed a bit embarrassed that he had called my father. I didn't say a word to him and the subject was never mentioned again.

It was obvious I wasn't going to leave Soho.

I went back downstairs and a punter came in. I sat talking to him. He was quite pleasant, a young man from the north of England who was studying and on a course in London for the weekend. Maggie brought the bill over; he had bought me two cocktails

Coke £4.95
Cocktail £85.00
Cocktail £85.00
Hostess fee £35.00

Subtotal £209.95

+ Service charge 27%

Total £266.63

This was a typical bill for a hostess bar. The punter paid and sat back down to wait for the show which Maggie was doing with Little Nicky. They were as funny as usual. As for the punter, I don't know whether he wanted to laugh or cry after paying all that money for a glass of cherryade and a coke.

Straight after that shift, when my dad had visited and I denied taking drugs; Maggie and I went out to find our dealer. He was called Jamie and he hung around Brewer or Berwick Streets. We paid £20 for a wrap of brown, then went home to have a smoke and enjoy the feeling of warmth that travelled round my body.

At that time we were probably each spending about £40 a day on heroin.
I had begun to notice that in the mornings, my legs would tingle if I hadn't got any. Then if I couldn't get any, the very next time I did have some, I would be violently sick. It was obviously becoming a problem. Maggie was the same, she was taking about the same amount but she never seemed to get sick or have a runny nose. I used to feel like I had flu. It didn't seem to have any effect on her if she couldn't

score. I would say at this time we weren't completely addicted to heroin but we were using a fair amount.

Life in the flat we rented from Little Ade in those early days was a strange experience. It was such a crazy time; the flat was always busy with people 'whizzing' or smoking cannabis or a bit of both. We used to love going to Little Ade's mad, pink flat for a visit. It was the thing to do before a night out in the West End. We all used to get wrecked in the flat - by the time we were ready to go out we would be chilled but a little paranoid. One of the girls we knew was a 'whiz-head' and always frantic. Another was very cool and organised. I just buzzed the whole time I was there. Ade always greeted us with a big smile and would then pass a joint which could have anything in it.
The flat always seemed to contain Scottish Ade, Maltese Martin, another Scottish Maggie (who spoke a million miles an hour in a thick Glasgow accent). I could hardly understand a word the woman said but it didn't really matter. I remember she never seemed to shut up. In hindsight it was the drugs she was on at the time. On the other hand there always seemed to be a silent woman on the end of the sofa. She was introduced as 'Max' and she never spoke. All she would do was just sit there staring at the telly. It didn't even have to be on; she would just sit there staring at it. I'm sure she sat there for a whole year just staring at the television. Everyone spoke to her but you would just get a distant nod in return if you were lucky.

We all seemed to talk at the same time, except for the silent one.
We would chat, joke and laugh, then out would come the marching powder, as we called cocaine, and then we would all be ready to go out. We seemed to float through the streets, nattering happily to each other, apart from her. She walked with us but in a trance-like state. On the odd occasion in The Fox, she might nod in time to the punk music that was booming out of the speakers but she never really spoke to anyone.

A while later, I was out with the gang in Loose Lips, a club we went to a fair bit. I was getting wasted as usual when the DJ put on an ACDC track called 'Highway to Hell'. Out of the blue, she broke her vow of silence and looked over at me.
'Do you want to dance?' she asked.

'Yes,' I said, surprised.

We went on the dance floor and head banged together. She was quite manic and didn't give a shit. We danced for ages. Then a girl with whom I'd had problems before came over, harassing me and trying to wind up the silent Max.
Max just lunged over the top of my shoulder and knocked the girl out. When we'd got over the shock and everything had settled down, she just grinned and said,

'The matter is now closed. Shall we get a drink?'

We became friends after that. I bumped into the other girl in The Fox shortly after that incident. She had two black eyes and a broken nose. She came over and said:

'Look what your girlfriend did to me!'

Max was with me at the time. She broke her silence again when the girl smiled at her. I will just say she didn't smile for too long.

# Hallucination

After about four years working at Maximillian's I moved on to work in other clubs. I was told there was big money to be made at clubs such as Erotica and Ambience but it was hard to get shifts in either of those places. Cassandra - 'Cass' was the older sister of Rene. She was blonde with big hair and loads of bounce and confidence. I found her a bit intimidating when I first met her. Cass was with a Maltese guy, Joe who didn't work in the West End, but stayed home looking after their kids. She had three children, two to Joe and one to a different man. None of the kids came down to the clubs. It was an unwritten rule that family life and the West End were kept very separate. Much later I went to Cass and Joe's wedding; a kilts only affair and a great day.

I didn't meet Cass until a few years after I had started working in the West End. She worked in a club that I'd never been to. I had seen her out and about but didn't know who she was at the time. I was told to watch my step with her as she didn't stand for any messing about. Cass was working the bar in Erotica when I went in to ask about a job there. As I walked inside Cassandra, in a broad Scottish accent, asked who I was and why I was in the club. I explained I was working with Rene at Maximillian's and looking for more work. She grunted something about new girls walking in and getting shifts then pointed to a short guy called Mike.

'Ask him,' she said.

She was a bit scary and also quite a lot bigger than her sister Rene. She could switch from nice to nasty in seconds. Mike said there were shifts available, but only working the door, there were no hostess shifts.

'You had better be good' Cass shouted over.

'We want loads of punters in, especially the Japanese!'

'Come upstairs with me,' Mike said and I followed him to the door.

'Give her half an hour, and see if she's any good!' Cass called after us.

So I sat on a door with music behind me shouting

'Live show sir! Sexy ladies!'

I did well, and was given the job. 17% of the bill that the punters paid was mine. It was so easy. Cass was impressed and I ended up getting quite a few shifts but only working the door.

I got on well with Cass after that - we became good friends. She still scared the shit out of me at times, but was always there for me.

I met a woman called Nancy at Erotica. She was married to a man everyone knew as Scouse Mike. He owned a West End video shop with another man from Liverpool. Nancy was like a mother figure to me and her sister Vonnie. I could do no wrong in her eyes and she was very protective of Vonnie. Anybody wanting to get close to her had to go through Nancy first.

Vonnie was always dressed to kill with perfect hair and make up. She had lived in Malta for many years and was married to a Maltese man. I used to think her life must be quite sad, because she kept how her husband made a living a secret for a long time. I found out that he played Blackjack in the casinos but had a special way of winning big money. I am not sure how he did it, but lets just say he wasn't winning the money fair and square. One night in Malta he had been up to his usual tricks and left the casino for home. He never made it. He had been rumbled. His body was found in an alleyway with a heroin needle sticking out of his neck.

His widow was left on her own with a young family to raise, so her sister Nancy invited her over to London. Vonnie worked the doors of the clubs on a regular basis. She was always concerned about how she looked, worrying if her hair was nice. She drank tea with a straw so that it wouldn't discolour her teeth. She was quite a nice person but had a very compulsive nature.

Sometime later Cassandra, Nancy and another woman opened their own club - Greens Court. Cass asked if I would come and do some shifts on the bar and as a hostess. I ended up near enough running Greens Court for them.

Cass and Joe got quite attached to taking cocaine in the last couple of years of me working there. Then they moved on to the new super drug, crack. He went from a stocky muscle man wearing loads of gold to a wafer thin shadow, destroying himself and his family.

I used to drop the takings off at Cassandra's after work as it was on my way home. One night, I dropped them off and Joe answered the door. He was holding a kitchen knife and high on crack. He asked me to come in. I was petrified but did go in; I was worried that he had hurt Cassandra or the kids.

When I got inside, all his tropical fish were taped one by one to the wall. He asked them, the fish, if Cass was having an affair.

I don't think he even realised I was there.

I looked for Cass and found her in the kitchen unharmed, but shaken. The house was a total mess. She sobbed that he had gone mad, pulled everything out of the cupboards and sliced the mattress, thinking there was a man hiding in there. All the time she was telling me this, Joe was shouting at the fish to tell him if she was being unfaithful.

When he finally calmed down a bit and sat down, I grabbed Cass and shoved her out of the door. Luckily the kids were at her sister Rene's, and I dropped her there. It had been a weird and very frightening experience.

Not long after that, Cass started using crack as well and slowly but surely all her gold started disappearing and so did the club.

# Chasing the Dragon

I was still living with Maggie in our little drug den. Our heroin consumption had increased - we were smoking it every day. The smell of heroin made me sick. As most of it was cut with glucose, it smelt sickly sweet, like burning sugar. At the side of my bed I kept a large plant pot. Every morning I would have my first smoke of the day and throw up into it, straight away.

Soho had been very quiet of late. The police were carrying out yet another campaign to try and close the clubs, trying to make tourists and visitors aware of what happened in them and prevent them from visiting. On one of my shifts I was only earning £30, which wasn't enough to support my habit. I met Maggie after work. She had been working as well, but hadn't earned half of what I had.
We needed more money for drugs.

She suggested we go 'clipping'. I had no idea what clipping was.

Maggie asked me what I thought the girls on the street were doing.
She meant the ones with short skirts, high heels and that were done up like they were going out for the night. I said I thought they were prostitutes.

'This isn't Kings Cross!' she said.

Unlike Kings Cross, Soho's prostitutes operated with set, but quite high prices, from the flats above the shops and businesses in the area.

'None of the girls who work the streets of Soho are prostitutes,' she laughed.

I was shocked. I seriously thought the girls and lads out on the streets were prostitutes. Then she said that we had to find some old keys. I was puzzled but helped her look for some.

When we were finally ready, we went out, and as we were walking I asked her what we were going to do. She said we were going to ask random men on the street if they wanted business, implying we were prostitutes. If they did we were to tell them how much and give them an old key.

I still didn't really understand but, I trusted her so went along with it. We got to

Brewer Street and hung around until Maggie spotted an unsuspecting tourist. She winked at me and moved in for the kill on a smart looking man. He was German, I think. Maggie moved up close to him and asked if he would like sex. He could have both of us if he wished.

On hearing that, he became very interested and kept looking me up and down. Maggie asked what he would like. He told her that he wanted a blow job from both of us. Maggie said it would be £70 and that he would have to pay us first.

'The police might be watching' she warned, looking round.

'So, while we walk round the block to put them off the scent, you go to number 12 Brewer Street and wait for us there.' She smiled sweetly.

I smiled too, thinking that no-one could be that gullible and that Maggie must be mad to try it on. But, he paid up and walked off happily clutching a useless key to the shop at number 12 Brewer St, while we went in the opposite direction.

He had been clipped.

Maggie said that we should nip into a pub for half an hour and give the probably irate man a chance to disappear.

'Then we can go back and it again,' she laughed.

We had a couple of drinks and went back out looking for another victim. We found one quite quickly but had to be careful. If we got caught by the clippers whose patch we were on, they would not be happy. We were taking money out of their pockets.

Maggie said it was my turn to have a go. I walked up to a likely punter and asked if he was looking for sex. My legs were like jelly. I was sure he would notice how much I was shaking, but he didn't seem to, just asked how much it would be for a blow job. I told him and then he asked how much for full sex. I told him £70. He nodded and agreed. I said we were being watched and so he had to meet us round the corner at an address and that he would have to pay first. He was unsure, but when I produced the key, it reassured him and he paid up.

I gave him the key, grabbed Maggie and we walked off to chase the dragon.

Clippers worked Soho night after night. We got to know most of them; quite a few were black girls. Maggie and I made friends with them all as it was better to have them on-side. There were a couple of transsexuals who were waiting to have sex changes. I found them a right laugh, but you could never trust them. Even though we became friends, they were into heroin in such a big way; we knew never to cross them. They weren't soft touches and it was common knowledge that many transsexuals working the streets carried knives.

My social life consisted of drinking in the local clubs and bars. On occasion, the girls from the clubs would all go out, together to a club called Miss Minnie's, which was an experience in itself. The hostesses were transvestites and the cabaret was men dressed as women singing or telling jokes to a very mixed audience that the acts wound up. We got to know most of the shows off by heart. It was always a good night out and the show would have everyone in stitches.

By that time I was working in three different clubs. I still did a few shifts at Maximillian's but I also worked at Greens Court and The Ambience Club which was right in the middle of Soho and run by a Maltese man and his wife. He was the grumpiest man I had ever met. He was making a fortune but hardly ever smiled. Working the door was good, but risky money as there was a greater chance of getting arrested for highway obstruction. It was there that I met 'Grey Beard' again. He was the top copper around Soho and his favourite arrest was for Obstruction of the Queen's Highway.

It was very difficult to keep a look out from the Ambience Club door. There was a market opposite and so many people were always passing by. Grey Beard just waited until it got busy and mingled in with the crowd then, when I started calling out to punters, he suddenly pounced. I couldn't believe my luck when he only gave me a warning.

Grey Beard had arrested me when I first started working in Soho and had taken an instant dislike to me, always waiting to catch me out. This time, he didn't seem to have recognised me from that first encounter. Although at the time I didn't think I had changed that much, with hindsight, I suppose I had grown up a lot since those early days in Soho and I had lost a lot of weight from all the drugs I was taking. He gave me the run down on the clubs and why I shouldn't be working in them. I think he was hoping I was really listening, and maybe, trying to make me feel as low as he could so I would go back to where I had come from.

His warning fell on deaf ears and I carried on calling 'live show'. I actually ended up having one of my best shifts ever; Maggie was working that day; we were going to The Fox after work, just by way of a change. We hadn't been out very much of late. Sitting at home chasing the dragon had taken over.

My work wasn't affected and I was getting a reputation as a good hostess and door girl and a lot of the Maltese club owners wanted me to work for them. Also, at that time there were a few clubs run by black guys on Great Windmill Street, but most of the girls who worked those clubs were druggies. On rare occasions, I would do a door or a show for them, if they paid me well enough that is.

A lot of these clubs were run by Elroy, he was fair but nobody messed with him or his 'brothers'. His clubs had a reputation for knocking punters about if paying the bill was an issue. To be fair though, all the clubs could get a bit rough at times. We all learned to look after ourselves very quickly, so we could fight back if we were attacked.

It was an unwritten rule of Soho that clubs shared their staff when needed and one day when I was working at Greens Court, Elroy came to ask if there were any spare girls, as two of his hadn't turned up for their evening shifts. It had been quiet at Greens Court and as his clubs were on one of the main thoroughfares through Soho, there was more chance of making money. I volunteered. It was a big risk working for these guys with a good chance of getting nicked if a punter brought the police back. Elroy's clubs were hated by the police and they loved the chance to arrest everyone in them.

Elroy's barman was a huge black man called Simon, six feet tall and as broad as he was long. A lovable big fellow, Simon became a close friend and "bodyguard' while I worked. If I needed protection he was always willing to help out, which could be useful in Soho.

I worked on the door and did some hostess work. True to his word Elroy paid me door commission and hostess commission. As I would have to deal with the punters I sent down I was probably more careful with them. I made them aware that they had to buy a drink and if they had a hostess sit with them they would have to pay more. But, they still came in and most of them paid up. I'm sure Simon's size swung it if there was an issue paying, which was funny Simon was a gentleman and such a softie; he just looked a bit of a monster.

The shift went well and we all made a good bit of money, Elroy was pleased and kept asking me to work more for him. I thanked him and said I had enough shifts at that time.

I also did take a couple of door shifts at a club called The Strip. It was on the main drag but was worked only by black girls. They didn't like a white girl on their patch and I felt quite intimidated at first, but my reputation for being good on the door helped me a little bit and they softened towards me once I had sent a few punters in.

There were three main girls who worked The Strip back then. Black Beryl, Yvonne and Yvette, they were all quite scary women if you didn't know them.

The Strip had a reputation for being very hard on the punters. Nobody got out without paying the bill - at any cost. They had men outside in case muscle was needed. It wasn't on most occasions however, the girls were frightening enough.

It was a busy club and hard work on the door. I had to keep groups of lads out and get the 'money punters' in. The best punters were Germans, Scandinavians, Japanese and Dutch who were usually on business with plenty of money or travellers cheques. We weren't fussy, money was money.

Americans were the hardest to get money out of and could get quite violent, pushing the girls around. They were also the most likely to come back with the police, which we tried to avoid at all costs. If they did come back with the police we had to either give them their money back or face arrest for demanding money with menaces, deception or robbery.

It was around this time I first met my slave. He wandered up to the Strip and paid to go in. Soon after he went downstairs I could hear the girls laughing and I went to see what they were laughing at. I took up position in the toilet and as I looked round the curtain used as a door, he was on his hands and knees cleaning the floor. I looked at the girls and they laughed at the look on my face. Yvette said he was a regular who paid well for the girls to force him to do horrible jobs. They used to tell him to crawl to the shop to buy them a beer. They would shout in his face that he was worthless and kick out at him as he crawled around on the floor. It was a turn on for him and he would say, 'thank you' nicely.
He carried on crawling about even when other punters came in. They laughed at him but he seemed to enjoy the torment. The worse people were to him the more he seemed to enjoy it. He would spend the whole shift in this way. On leaving, he would bow and praise the girls, or 'madams' as he called them.
Then, he'd tidy himself up and go back to his office.

We had some odd punters. Most of them would walk in and you would never see them again. But we did have a few regulars, who would visit every time they were in London on business.

The Strip had one who came in regularly. A very tall man in his 50's and very smartly dressed. He worked in the City but lived up north coming into the club once a month for three days when he was on business in the City.

He liked Yvette and would come in to see her. His thing was to dress up as a woman. Yvette would help him put on his make-up and hair, at a price of course. Then he would ask for a cup of tea in a china cup and saucer and sit in the club talking to the girls about make-up and clothes.
He would bring a bag of his own clothes with him, mainly tights and underwear. The girls would tell him what a good looking, sexy, woman he was. Like the slave, he would then just tidy himself up and go back to work in the city.

Mostly, punters just wanted to see scantily dressed girls. With the club being called 'The Strip' they expected strip-shows but unless they paid a huge bill with extra fees they got nothing for their money. That could cause problems for me as they made their way out. They would shout at me for ripping them off, threatening to come back and kill us all, that sort of thing.

On one shift we had a German punter who didn't like black girls but wanted to come in anyway, insisting that I was to be his hostess. He asked for Yvette and me to do the show together. He confessed he liked black girls sexually, but was scared of them. He bought me cocktail after cocktail but never really looked at me while we were talking. He couldn't keep his eyes of Yvette and Yvonne. I suggested that while I stayed with him he could be brave and let Yvette come and sit with us for a cocktail. He agreed. Trying to persuade this grown man that black girls were harmless was like dealing with a child scared of the bogeyman.

Yvette was very sweet to him but when Yvonne brought the bill over he said he was only prepared to pay for my company. Yvonne lost her cool and started shouting at him and accused him of being racist. The man started crying and told us that his grandmother was black and he had been tormented by the fact for years. Then he paid up and left.

Working in the clubs could be very entertaining. Every day was so very different. I really enjoyed my time in the West End clubs. It was a different way of life and I am glad to have experienced it. Some aspects were not so nice though and there were some very odd people about with some serious issues.

There were a lot of private flats above and opposite Greens Court club and, when I was working on the door I would see young boys coming in and out of one flat in particular. I assumed it was a drug thing. They always looked so sad, these young lads. The man who owned the flat was a short, fat man with greasy hair, repulsive and rude.

I was standing on the door one morning and suddenly heard lots of shouting from the flats. As I looked out, a young man, who looked like one of the street boys who slept in boxes under the arches or on the doorways, was trying to get out of the door and the fat man was preventing him. He finally got away and as he walked off, the repulsive little fat man was hanging out of his window shouting abuse at him. The boy looked terrified.

As he walked past me I could see he had been crying and was in a right mess. His white jeans were covered in blood at the back. He got as far as the end of Greens Court before he hit the ground, unconscious. I ran towards him and people gathered around. One of the men from the club called the police and an ambulance. They arrived very quickly and took him to hospital.

The police came to the door to ask what I had seen.

I told them that all I saw was the fat man shouting abuse at the boy as he was walking away. We didn't hear anything for a while, but one of the other men who lived in the flats called by the club one day and said the boy was a young street urchin the fat man had picked up. He had promised him a roof for the night and a bit of comfort. As soon as the lad had gone back he had raped him and shoved a broom handle up his back passage.

Realistically, the young street lad couldn't help the police to press rape and assault charges against the fat man, so he was free to continue his sick and debauched attacks luring vulnerable young boys up to his hellhole to satisfy his sick needs.

The saddest thing is that was they were just young men who needed a bit of love and to be looked after. That evil bastard preyed on them. This was one of the horrible sides to Soho and it went on all the time.

Around this time I had started to see Irish Don who I had met through Little Ade. Don was a funny man from Northern Ireland. We'd met many times in Ade's pink flat but never really bothered with each other, we exchanged small talk but that was about it.

On one of our nights out, our usual gang gathered at Ade's then went to The Fox and on to a rock club. The clubs were all rock in the Soho area at that time. The Marquee Club was a favourite for live bands.
The night was going quickly and we were all having a great time dancing to Bon Jovi and other 80s rock. Don was with a very odd French girl at the time that none of our crowd liked. I asked if he wanted to join us for a dance.

It sort of started from there.

We danced for ages and then found ourselves kissing. At this point the French girl reappeared and groped at Don.

Bang! She was on the floor.

I'd hit her.

This was out of character for me as in those days I was so chilled out with the various drugs I was taking. There was mayhem for a while with the bouncers rushing about all over the club, not quite knowing what to do. They were used to drunken fights between blokes, but this was two women. One was on the floor and the other, me, had gone back to having a drink and a dance.
The bouncers knew me quite well and it was the French girl who was asked to leave. She was glad to.

I guess I had sort of claimed him now.

Don asked if I wanted to go back to his place for a smoke. I was happy with that and he asked Maggie to join us. With the offer of more drugs she, of course, said yes. We got to Don's in Willesden Green, a big Irish area.
He lived with two women. One was completely nuts, always on speed and rushing

around like a maniac. The other one was quite sensible; she worked in the music industry but she was also always on some kind of drug. Drugs were a big thing in those days. That first night we spent listening to music and smoking weed. When it was time to get some sleep, Don suggested Maggie and I both get in with him.

Threesomes were not my thing and he was soon told it wasn't going to happen.

I still wind him up to this day about his generous offer that night. Maggie slept on the sofa and we all got some sleep. After Maggie went to work the next day Don and I chilled together listening to music. He asked me then if I would like to move in.

As mad as it must sound, I agreed.

We stayed together for fourteen years.

# Your Missus is a Nutter

I moved in with Don, but I still worked my shifts and knocked around with Maggie. Don had a good job with BritishTelecom, but was also the DJ for the Marquee, a big rock club. I used to walk down to meet him in the club after work to see live bands and attend the club's parties.
I got on with one of the girls (the mad one) that he shared the flat with quite well. She was called Annie and she sometimes came out with us in the West End.

After a while, she got together with Little Ade. It was a strange and very fiery combination. The two of them were so similar; they were either very in love or wanted to kill each other. Annie was a good laugh and we often went to The Fox together waiting for the others. Don would arrive on his motorbike and we would all party.

I had kept my heroin addiction a secret from Don. I just did my own thing with it. I was still taking quite a big amount and also taking speed and smoking joints all the time. I hid the heroin at home in the bath panel and took speed straight after to make sure my eyes were not pinned. The pupils of the eyes diminish to pin-pricks when you have taken heroin, it is one of the first things anyone with experience of the drug notices when they meet a user. Taking speed counteracts this effect.

I knew from Ade that Don was anti-heroin, but was alright about cocaine. It's strange when you look back, at what was acceptable and what wasn't. It was perfectly acceptable to clean coke into crack and smoke that, but not to smoke heroin.

I kept my habit from him for quite a while. I was very sneaky, but I got away with it as money wasn't an issue. I could afford whatever I needed. It would only be a problem if I couldn't get any or I ran short of money.

Soon after I moved in with Don, Cassandra, an owner of Greens Court came into the club to see how her girls were doing and to invite us to a surprise party for one of her partners, Nancy, and her husband. Laughing, she told us she had booked a stripper dressed as a black priest for Nancy, a Maltese Catholic, and a roly-poly strip-o-gram for Scouse Mike, her husband. She was pleased when we all said we would come.

I told Don about the party and said if he would like to go to it we could, so we went to The Fox and met up with the gang. I popped out with Maggie to get some heroin and we found our dealer. He seemed on edge and warned us to be careful. He was suspected by many to be a grass, but his gear was good. We followed him for a while down narrow alleyways and bought some wraps of heroin. Just as he was about to hand them over we were jumped on by three plainclothes police officers. They had been waiting to pounce, but did so just a second before he had handed it over. He had got our money but we hadn't got the drugs.

They took us to Vine Street police station and searched us for the heroin. We were lucky. They carried out a thorough strip-search on us both but they couldn't find any. But, Maggie had borrowed my jacket earlier to go to the shop. She had left half a joint and some weed in a match box in one of the pockets. The police were almost jumping up and down when they found it. They had got me for something, even if it wasn't what they wanted to do me for.

I could have killed Maggie. I had been so cocky with them for screwing up and now, because of her, they had something on me. They kept me as long as they could, and eventually gave me a caution, but they weren't that happy as they had expected to do us for so much more, but had timed it all wrong.

We got out of the station relatively unscathed, but we were desperate. We had no heroin and had lost all our money. We walked back to The Fox hardly speaking, anxious and miserable, and already sniffing with withdrawal symptoms. We had been gone about four hours. Don was stood by the door wondering where we had been, but I was definitely not in the mood for a load of questions, especially with no drugs. I told him we had called into one of the clubs, they were short staffed and so we'd stood in.

He accepted this and carried on with his pint. Maggie looked round The Fox to see if anyone could help us out. There was nobody in there we knew that would supply us with heroin. She even went round to people we didn't know to see if there was anything going but there was nothing.

Maggie left and Don and I went home. My nose was running and I was sniffing constantly. I hoped Don just thought I was coming down with something. Then, he didn't know the signs of withdrawal from heroin.

After a night of no sleep I felt awful. My legs hurt and my nose was dripping like a tap and I was so irritable. Don went to work and I met Maggie who looked and felt as bad as I did.

This was my first time of feeling what cold turkey might be like.

Maggie had managed to borrow some money from her brother; we almost ran for a taxi and headed south of the river to a very dodgy looking estate.

'We can get sorted here,' she said.

The flat was very smart and tidy. The dealer, an old friend of her ex, was Greek, pleasant and knew Maggie very well. They disappeared and left me sitting in the flat, which I found a bit scary. The half an hour they were gone seemed more like three.

When they came back, he reached under the table and got a huge bag of brown powder out. He put a pile on the table and said help yourselves.
I looked at Maggie and she just smiled at me. Maggie helped herself to a large amount of the heroin and put some on a bit of foil.

I threw up on mine straight away, but my nose stopped running, the shivers stopped and the horrible pains went away. We both felt a lot better after our session. He called us a cab; we thanked him and left taking a large wrap each away with us.

Maggie and I didn't really speak much about the Greek man or her disappearing with him. I don't quite know where they went or what they did, but I think she had an arrangement with him of sex for heroin if she was desperate.

In a much better mood, I went to work at Greens Court. I was doing a hostess shift that day and my first punter was an American, who for once, settled his bill with no argument. He bought me two cocktails and himself a beer. We talked for ages and he saw the show; one of the other girls wriggling around on the bed, and he left quite happily. My next punter was Japanese. He ordered drinks for everyone and paid a huge bill, including a made-up booking fee. He didn't want to see a show, he was just happy to sit with ladies by his side, talking.

He was quite a nice punter but we had some bad punters in after that. 'Table jumpers', we called them.

The bar person would take the bill and table jumpers, if they were quick, would leap across the low table and run up the stairs as fast as they could. This could be amusing when they ran the wrong way and ended up in the toilet, they were trapped then and we had them.

Just before the end of the shift, one of the girls had another Japanese man in. Like the first, he ordered drinks for everyone and ran up a huge bill. The bar person had gone home early so I gave him the bill. He was very charming and paid in American dollars. He watched the show and seemed very happy. We finished the shift off, the girls came in for the evening shift and we all left.

Maggie met me from work and we walked round to The Fox to meet the rest of the gang. As we were upstairs having a beer and relaxing, we looked out of the window. There was a lot of police around, more than normal and they seemed to be looking for someone. We sat watching them, laughing and drinking beer for about an hour then one of the club's evening shift girls came in asking for me.

It was Toni and she looked worried. The last punter we had served, the nice Japanese man, had brought the police back to the club and claimed I had hit him and stolen his money out of his wallet. The amount he was claiming I had taken was a lot more than he had actually paid. He was obviously being told what to say by the police, which wasn't unheard of in the West End then.

The bosses had been there when he came back and not only were the police looking for me, but the bosses wanted me to explain, why, if he had paid that much money it wasn't on the sheet.

The police we had been watching were looking for me, on charges of robbery, blackmail, deception and demanding money with menaces. I was in deep trouble.

The guy had said he was staying for two more days so he could well come back to the club in that time to identify me. I also knew the police would love the fact someone wanted to go ahead and press charges and would push it. My other concern was that the bosses thought I had robbed them.

Toni advised me to stay in The Fox until things calmed down and promised she would get the girls from the morning shift to tell the bosses how much he had really paid. I thanked her and she left me to stay where I was until the streets were clear of police. Then I went to meet Don, I told him what had happened and we agreed that I should stay out of Soho for a few days. I asked him to go to Greens Court to see the bosses for me.

My biggest problem now was my habit. Staying out of Soho meant I couldn't score any heroin. The next morning the shivers and leg cramps started. I knew I would need him so I asked Don not to go into work. I decided to sit him down and come clean about my drug problems.

He was so horrified. I thought it was the end of us. But, he was good about it all and said he would help me get off the heroin and sort my life out. He would be there for me. I agreed, but of course that was easy when I couldn't get any and was away from the only place I knew where to score. Would it be that simple to stay off it when I was back where heroin and the money for it were so readily available?

I think he was more shocked that I had kept it secret for so long. I was surprised that he hadn't guessed, but with him smoking weed all the time and taking cocaine, our lives were always a bit of a blur, neither of us was ever straight in those days.

*Rupert St, Soho, remnants of the sex industry still coexist alongside the theatres and retail outlets of Soho.*

*Wardour St, Soho. New, more acceptable businesses have replaced the old as Soho tries to shed its old, seedy image.*

*The imposing West End Central Police Station, where I was taken on a number of occasions*
(picture reproduced by kind permission of Tottenham and Bennett)

*The bar area of Maximillian's, as you can see no expense was spared on the decor.*

## Lager/Lager & Lime

| ½ Pint | £4.00 |
| Pint | £8.00 |

## Shandy

| ½ Pint | £4.00 |
| Pint | £8.00 |

## Soft Drinks

| Cola | £4.00 |
| Lemonade | £4.00 |
| Mineral Water | £4.00 |
| Fruit Juice | £4.00 |

## House Wine

Red or White
- Glass £12.50
- Bottle £50.00

Service charge & V.A.T 27½%
V.A.T. Number

*All drinks, by law, de-alcoholised*

## House Wine

Red or White
- Glass £12.50
- Bottle £50.00

## Cocktails

| Erotic dream | £40.00 |
| Lady's delight | £60.00 |
| Mirage Special | £90.00 |

## Champagne

(Sparkling Wine) £125.00

A seated conversation with a hostess is an acceptance to pay the full fee/bill for the drinks, company, service and V.A.T. The first drink purchased for or from a Hostess warrants the additional charge of the hostess fee. All cocktails are available in single or double measures. Regular customers are charged only £25.00 for any cocktail. Once the bill has been paid in full, (including hostess fee), drinks for customers are free of charge. No further charge will be made for company or shows. The customer may then remain on the premises until he decides to leave, or until closing time, (Whichever is the earliest). Customers who do not engage the company of a hostess, are requested to leave the premises after one show. No service is available at the bar. Hostess service only.

**Hostess Fee £35.00**
(Additional charge for first drink purchased for/from a hostess)

Service charge & V.A.T 27½%
V.A.T. Number

*All drinks, by law, de-alcoholised*

**BEARER** *(Titulaire)*
Name **MISS MAXINE ANN WHITE**
*Nom*

Address in United Kingdom **76 WHITE HART LANE**
*Domicile*
**LONDON**                Post Code **N17 8HP**

Date and place of birth **NOTTINGHAM**
*Date et lieu de naissance*

Height **1.57m**    Distinguishing marks **TATTOO'S**
*Taille*            *Signes particuliers*

**SPOUSE** *(Epouse/Epoux)*
Name
*Nom*

Date and place of birth
*Date et lieu de naissance*

Height              Distinguishing marks
*Taille*            *Signes particuliers*

**CHILDREN** *(Enfants)*
Name *(Nom)*    Date of birth *(Date de naissance)*    Sex *(Sexe)*

---

*Photograph of spouse*

Signature of bearer *Maxine*
*Signature du titulaire*

Signature of spouse
*Signature de son épouse/époux*

**WARNING TO HOLDER**

Before making a journey abroad with this passport you should check that it is:—
(a) Still in force and will not expire before you return.
(b) Valid for the countries you propose to visit or travel through (see page 3).

---

## COUNTRIES FOR WHICH THIS PASSPORT IS VALID

| | |
|---|---|
| ANDORRA | DENMARK (includes Faroe Islands, Greenland) |
| AUSTRIA | |
| BELGIUM | FINLAND |
| FRANCE (includes Corsica) | ICELAND |
| GERMANY | NORWAY |
| GIBRALTAR | SWEDEN |
| ITALY (includes Sicily, Sardinia, Elba) | Visits to this group of countries as a whole must not exceed 3 months in any 9 month period. |
| LIECHTENSTEIN | |
| LUXEMBOURG | GREECE (includes Greek Islands) |
| MALTA | TURKEY |
| MONACO | But *not* valid for travel to Greece or Turkey by overland route through other adjacent countries. |
| NETHERLANDS | |
| PORTUGAL (includes Madeira, Azores) | |
| SAN MARINO | BERMUDA |
| SPAIN (includes Balearic and Canary Isles) | But *not* valid for any visits to the United States of America. |
| SWITZERLAND | |
| TUNISIA | |

*The site of the Greenscourt Club.*

*Don and my unconventional 'Motorbike Wedding'.*

The next couple of days were filled with pain and sniffles. I felt sick all the time and the only thing that got me to sleep was Night Nurse. I drank half a bottle and it knocked me out.

Don called down to Greens Court and spoke to the bosses. The girls that had worked with me on that shift told them how much the punter had really paid, so they knew he was lying. They asked Don to reassure me that things would be fine when I decided to go back to work. I could go back when I was ready to, but that the police had been down to the club several times with the punter to identify me and take me in.

This was a reality check.

I finally realised how dangerous Soho was……..sort of.

I went back to Greens Court for my first shift after all the excitement had died down. Maggie popped in to see how I was doing as I hadn't contacted her for a while. There were no mobile phones around then. I could see she was stoned, she looked a bit sweaty and her eyes were like pin pricks. Seeing her brought on a strong urge for some heroin, but when I asked her for some, she refused. She was trying to get off it too.

It was nearly time for Mike and Nancy's party. It was to be the following Saturday night. We were all looking forward to it. Unfortunately the club would still be open and I was on a late shift that night. Of course no-one wanted to swap shifts with me, so I would have to join the party later on.

It was already busy when we arrived. Before long it was time for the big event and Rene asked everyone to be quiet. In came this big black priest. He headed straight towards Nancy, stripped off his cassock and gyrated to the music, grabbing at her; she nearly died of embarrassment.

Everyone was in stitches except for Nancy. The terrified look on her face amused everyone even more. Just as it all calmed down; in came Crazy Jane, the roly-poly strip-o-gram. She was huge, and made her way straight towards her victim, Mike.

She was wearing the tiniest bikini and had just layers and layers of fat hanging over the bikini. She waddle-danced over and tried to sit on his knee. He jumped up to escape but she wouldn't let him, he had to dance. It was so funny; him swearing like mad in Maltese made it even funnier. The party was really lively now, the drinks were flowing and everyone was having a good time. It did seem a bit odd partying out of the West End but with everyone from the West End. It wasn't my sort of party but I was enjoying myself. It was the 80s, the clothes were bright and there was a lot of big hair. The music wasn't bad and everyone was dancing, drinking and chatting.

Everyone was there. Annie, a girl I had worked with and her sister were there too. Annie's sister 'Mad' Esther was a bit 'worse for wear' staggering about and annoying people until finally, Rene went over and said it was perhaps time she went home. Mad Esther stared at Rene drunkenly for a few moments without saying anything then staggered over to the little stage where the DJ was.

She asked him for the microphone, the music was turned down. We waited. She shouted over the mike that on more than one occasion, Rene had shagged Mike and that once, Rene had been giving Mike a blow job while he was on the phone with Nancy. The room fell silent. Then Rene flew at Esther; Nancy flew at Rene, and Mike and Dougie were having it out. The fighting spilled out of the little house and into the street.

No-one else moved, everybody was at a loss as to what to say or do. It was shocking; everything had all gone wrong in a matter of seconds. A couple of us went to see if Nancy was okay. She had run into the toilet and was sobbing. She was saying she knew it was true, she knew Mike was always messing around with other women. I did feel for her, it was like the old song 'It's my party'. Someone managed to get Rene and Dougie into one taxi and the drunken Mad Esther into another. She was still shouting manically that there was more to be said and calling Rene all sorts of names. The party died a quick death as taxis arrived to take people home. Don and I left.

What a mess it all was. These people worked together, they would all have to face each other again. I just wondered what would happen now at the club. Mad Esther did shifts on our door, luckily Rene didn't work any shifts there. She did all her shifts at Erotica but Nancy was one of its bosses. It would all be very uncomfortable for a good while to come. On the surface, things seemed to have moved on. The events at the party were not mentioned. I think we all wanted to forget it, but there was an underlying tension around for a long while.

Shortly after all this had happened, I was on the door of Greens Court one Saturday night, near closing time. Suddenly I could hear lots of yelling and shouting around the corner in an alleyway and then a deathly quiet. I shouted down to the girls to watch the door for me and I ran up the alleyway to see what was going on.

I couldn't see anything, just the normal Saturday night drinkers and party goers; I went back on my door. Later, just as I was about to lock up, Nancy's Mike staggered down the alley, covered in blood. He was in a right mess. I ran up to him and helped him get into the club. I thought he was going to pass out. When he had sat for a while and calmed down I asked what had happened. Mike was no soft touch; he was from Liverpool and could look after himself, so it was a bit of a shock to say the least that he was in such a mess.

Apparently he had been drinking with friends in the Red Lion, the pub he always went in. He was on his way to fetch the takings from me, but was followed and attacked with bike chains. I asked if he knew who had done it. He just nodded that yes he did. We walked him down to catch a taxi and he went home. This is what the West End was like, it was always buzzing. Everyday there was always something happening.

It later emerged that the nasty attack on Mike was down to the events at the party. It was a couple of Maltese who had attacked him with the bike chains. It wasn't just the fact that he had messed about with Rene, who was with a Maltese man. Nancy was also half Maltese and he had cheated on her.

No-one ever found out who had done it or who they had specifically done it for. They had beaten him all the way up the road with metal bike chains, kicking him as they went. All this was done in full view of the door staff of different clubs but no-one had helped him. He had done wrong and was dealt with.

Around this time, I was back on heroin and using my old trick of taking speed so that Don wouldn't notice my pin-prick eyes. Maggie was using more than ever. It was getting close to Christmas and we needed to sort out enough to get us both through the holiday period.

I was supposed to be going home to Uttoxeter. Maggie was going back to Glasgow and Don was going back to Northern Ireland to see his children. The police stepped up their campaign of getting the dealers off the streets at this time of the year, they were also warning punters about the illegal activities of the clip joints, as the clubs were called.

Maggie and I worked the last few shifts together. I ended up with a bruised face and twisted ankle courtesy of an American. Maggie had sat with him and I took the bill over. At first he was fine and paid the bill. I put some sexy music on and he paid extra for Maggie and me to do the show together. We danced around him and did a bit of a saucy lap dance. The shows were sexual but we didn't actually touch each other. He really enjoyed the show and disappeared into the toilet for obvious reasons. When he came out another punter was getting his bill and the American realised he had been ripped off.

He grabbed Maggie by the hair and was shouting abuse at her. I went in to get him off her and he stuck his arm out with a big clenched fist that connected with my eye. He shoved me across a table and ran up the stairs, nearly knocking the door girl out on his way out. It shook us both up a bit as the bloke had been so calm and seen a show. We expected a bit of bad behaviour when the bill was first taken across but not such a long time after it had been paid.

We closed up. We needed to get some heroin but no-one was around, so Maggie suggested we go to South London to visit her Greek friend. He wasn't in. I was getting really stressed by this stage and needed, badly, to get some gear. We walked to a phone box to try his number. He answered; he was at home but hadn't answered the door as he was being watched. He came out and we met him in a taxi rank. We did the deal and he gave us a little extra as Maggie was a bit special to him. As we went away in the taxi we looked back at him through the rear window and he waved at us.

That was the last time we saw him. The very same night the police raided his flat and found a huge amount of heroin and some weapons. They arrested our friend and took him in to the police station.

Within twenty four hours he was dead; apparently he had committed suicide in police custody. The police claimed he was embarrassed about his family finding out and couldn't do the time he was looking at in prison.

We were both upset when we found out, whether it was because of his death and how he died or because we wouldn't be able to obtain drugs from him anymore I really couldn't say.

In those days people came and went in your life all the time. Life went on and someone else would appear sooner rather than later doing exactly the same thing. Nothing ever changed in the West End, just the faces.

I often phoned home at this point, and always rang my surrogate baby brother, John, to catch up on gossip from back home. We have always been close, still are, he is godparent to my son and we never go a fortnight without talking to each other. John is very shy and very easy going. When he met his first girlfriend, he brought her round to meet me, to see what I thought of her.
On this day John had some bad news for me. Our childhood friend Kev had died in an accident with a chainsaw. Kev was messed up with all the substances he had been taking. He was a heroin addict, that also took amphetamines and he had suffered a mental breakdown following the break up of his relationship.
He was filling a chainsaw up with petrol while smoking a cigarette. He spilt petrol all over the chainsaw and all over himself. Suddenly, he was consumed in a ball of flames.
His life was very sad. He had been devastated after his partner, the love of his life, had left him and then to suffer such a death, at so young an age, was tragic. The way he was taken was horrific to anyone who knew and loved him.
It hit me like a hammer blow. Kev had always been one of our gang while we were growing up. It didn't help my drug addiction. I sought refuge in what I knew would numb my feelings, the tin foil, the straw and the dangerous but wonderful brown sticky substance called heroin. Every addict looks for every excuse possible to indulge in their habit.

I didn't go to the funeral; it just went clean out of my mind.

# Peep Show

Don and I had been seeing each other for a couple of years by this point. I still worked the clubs; he was still DJ at The Marquee. We spent lots of nights watching the bands, then drinking and socialising with them in the green room. There were some huge bands out and about in the 80s. It was all very glam and the Marquee was always rocking.

It had got very quiet in Soho, a lot of the club owners were moaning about the lack of punters. If we didn't make much on our shift, I went back to a bit of clipping with Maggie There were always gullible men who were more than willing to part with their cash for what they thought was going to be the sexual adventure of their lives.

Clipping always made me feel nervous but the drugs helped.
At the time, Maggie and I felt indestructible, we knew no real fear.
We didn't really think about what we were doing, or who we were hurting.
The approach, the talk, and then dodging the punter and the police made the adrenaline surge through my body.
It was a huge buzz.

We had become good friends with most of the clippers and they didn't seem to mind too much if we went out on their patch, unlike the prostitutes of Kings Cross. New girls that appeared on their turf had a big problem. In those days a lot of the prostitutes carried a knife and most would pull them on another prostitute and if they didn't, their pimp would do it for them.

The strange thing about Soho was that I could walk round it any time of the night or day without fear. In most cities you would think twice about doing the same thing. We all looked out for each other and it really was an extended family.

I don't know who thought the clipping thing up, but it was very clever, girls giving over a key for a large amount of money and giving nothing in return. Clippers all looked the part, of course. Some of them were sex change hopefuls waiting on their operations, like those I had met in Kings Cross.
They had no fear as they were men ripping off men. I worked alongside one of these guys one night and had the time of my life. He was Irish from Dublin, very tall but a believable woman, looking better than me. He had legs to die for and was one of the best clippers in the business. His name was Ricky. He had a Glaswegian

boyfriend who was a heroin dealer and a fantastic shop lifter. He could get anything that anyone wanted and sold to order in the clubs.

At that time there were a lot of thieves operating around the West End. They would steal to order for the girls in the clubs. They knew the girls who worked the clubs always had money. One day, a lad came down and I asked him to go to Ann Summers and get me a bag full of sexy clothes in size 14 or 44 DD. It was for work so I wanted everything lacy; bras, knickers, stockings. Basques or all in ones were fine and everything should be red or black, my favourite colours for underwear.

After about an hour he returned with a black bin bag full of underwear. He wanted £20 for the lot. That sort of thing happened all the time and we ordered anything from clothing to weekend bags and fresh meat.

Both Ricky and his boyfriend had big heroin habits. Ricky worked in the alleyway close to The Strip, clipping, nearly every night. Quite a few clippers worked the same area. Maggie hadn't been around lately so I asked Ricky if he minded me doubling up with him. Clippers always worked in pairs for safety.

Ricky was a funny person with an amazing personality. He had me in stitches all night. He took the piss out of the punters while he was clipping them. Acting in a very camp manner, he spoke pure filth to them and would go into graphic detail of what the punter would get for his money. Then he would have a little giggle to himself. They would be getting nothing but an empty wallet.

He gave me a lesson to start with.

'Watch and learn,' he said.

He instructed me to put on my nicest, if falsest smile.

'Act sweet and innocent,' he said.

'And if they ask give a false name.'

He introduced himself as Sabrina to a punter and asked if he would like to have an enjoyable time. He moved up close alongside them, a hair's breadth away from brushing himself up against their groin area. This tease got them visibly interested and he had them eating out of his hand. Then he moved in for the kill. Speaking very quietly, almost whispering, he told them what he would be able to do for them.

This punter was just an average looking man in his 40s. No doubt he was married. He didn't want anything kinky, a blow job from both of us then straight sex with Ricky. All for a fee of just £85, which Ricky said was the key money for his private room in the flats. Ricky didn't have to do any more coaxing. He just showed the punter where he was to meet us and exchanged the key for the money.

While the punter found out that the key didn't fit the lock and he wasn't getting Ricky or me for his money, off we skipped for a coffee. I didn't feel anxious around Ricky, I felt safe with him. I think it was his confidence. He was a man and could look after himself, even dressed to kill as a woman.

We left it about half an hour and went back out to look for our next victim. It was quite exciting. Our next punter was a big African, but Ricky whispered to me we had to fuck him off as they were too violent and never gave up looking for the clippers who had taken their money. He was a big man in his late 30s and he had an unpleasant smell.

Ricky asked him what he would like, but whatever it was the man wanted he was going to have to find someone else who could provide the service for him. I didn't like him, he was creepy. He smirked at us and licked his lips. He was repulsive and even if I had been a prostitute I would have refused this one.

He asked Ricky what his favourite sexual act was, hoping to get a cheap thrill. But Ricky replied in a sharp, short cutting manner.

'Sorry but you will have to find someone else as you are now asking for anal sex without a condom with us both.'

Not the answer he had been waiting for. He had no money either, so we excused ourselves and left him.

The man shouted up the street after us and it became a bit scary, he was calling us slags and bitches and anything else he could think of but we were soon out of his sight, much to my relief; such an unpleasant character.

As we had wasted so much time with the dreadful African, we decided to stay out for a little while longer, hoping to get one last gullible punter. Before long, we pounced on a very nice German man. He was young, very good looking and you could tell by his clothes and the way he held himself that he was not short of money. I wondered why he would need to pay for any sexual service. Maybe it was just the thrill of it all. He wanted straight sex, no frills and nothing strange. He accepted that he would need to pay for the flat key as security and that it would be £150 and paid up no problem.

Ricky thought he would push his luck with this punter and asked him if he would like something extra and see both of us in a lesbian show before his sexual encounter. His eyes lit up and his voice went to a higher pitch. He almost whispered to Ricky that he would like that. Ricky whispered back that it would be another £100. The German couldn't wait to pay him. Ricky winked at me and handed me the key to the non-existent flat. I motioned to the punter to follow behind me and led him up the alleyway towards some flats. I told him to walk round the block in case the police were watching. We would both be ready and waiting for him on his return.

We were more than happy with our nights work. Ricky thanked me for working with him and said that we worked well together. We went our separate ways, leaving the punter still eagerly waiting in anticipation as we got into our taxis.

It had been a good night for money and all had gone well. I got safely home to Don and for once we had a night in, just relaxing.

The next day I was working at Greens Court and Little Ade came to see me. He had organised a night out when he was stoned and booked tickets to see Frank Sinatra live with Liza Minnelli, which made me laugh.

He asked if I fancied going with them to see it for a giggle, but I said no, a couple of hours listening to that did nothing for me. He had already spoken to Don who had accepted. Fine, Don could go without me. The concert was at the Royal Albert Hall, full of oldies all suited and booted. In the middle of them all would be Ade, Don - a biker with long red hair who wore a bandana, a leather jacket and jeans - and nutty Ann who was always whizzing round like a lunatic and couldn't keep quiet for five minutes.
They were to arrive in Ade's uncle's big Rolls-Royce.
It was too bizarre.

But, the main reason Ade had visited was to ask me if I would do a peep show shift, the clubs were revamping the peep shows to boost trade. It took him a good half hour to persuade me to have a go. In the end I agreed to try it but only if I liked what I was doing. I was to do the late shift the following day.
After he left and as it was quiet in the club, I helped out in the video shop next door. It was quite odd. Punters froze if there was a woman behind the counter. It seemed to make them very uncomfortable and a couple of them went out without buying anything, too embarrassed to ask a female for whatever kinky stuff they wanted to buy.

Having said that, one man did ask me for a video of a woman having a shit on a glass table. I was nearly sick but found the one he was looking for. I'm sure that he enjoyed seeing my reaction. It was so strange what some people were into. When the man who ran the shop came back, I told him what had happened and he laughed. He told me that golden showers, people urinating on each other, and shit, or scat videos were very popular. Next in popularity came all the lesbian stuff. I won't say I was shocked, as the longer I worked in and around the sex industry the more I learned. I learnt something new every day.

When I finished work I met Don in The Fox and we went to see Alice Cooper playing at the Marquee Club. His floor show was supposed to be very different and well

worth a look. We had a great night out and yes, the show was very different to any I had seen before. There were live snakes on stage and Alice had a guillotine which he said was to chop his own head off. It was quite a strange experience. I didn't drink a great deal when I was out at any time. My thing was always drugs and getting the ultimate high.
My rock and roll lifestyle fitted in well with Soho and its rock scene at that time.

The following day I went into work. It was very quiet, the door girl was moaning and everyone was grumpy. Every punter who came in seemed to have no money and if they did there were big fights to try and get them to part with it. We'd had a few days like that. It was very frustrating and everyone got bitchy with each other. Finally, we had a breakthrough. A punter came in and requested my company. He bought me several cocktails and asked for another hostess to join us. He paid the bill without any argument and we sat chatting. He was Austrian and was in London on business. He told me that when he had got off the plane, he was given a flyer by uniformed police warning him of the evils of Soho. We realised then, why it had been so quiet. Punters were being scared off at the airports before we could trap them in the clubs. They already knew what was going to happen to them if they went inside clubs like ours.

It was my first peepshow. It was all very new to me and I didn't really understand what I was meant to do. Ade met me and explained that it was a vibrator show which was performed behind glass. There was a peep box with a slit in it for money. Every pound the punter put in got them three seconds. It was just enough time for a smile and a pose, the bigger the tip the better the performance. The punter got to see nothing special until the money really flooded through the slit.

The girls got a percentage of their tips plus the peep money. On a reasonable shift they could earn anything from £200 to around £600, so it was easy money really. I did finish my shift but I didn't like it and knew pretty quickly that it wasn't for me. I made some very good money, but I found it just too degrading. You were there, sitting or lying in a box using a vibrator on yourself while men stood on the other side of the glass, playing with themselves.

There was a man called the 'spunk monitor', and he went in the peep booth as soon as it emptied and mopped up the spunk which the punters had left on the floor. I found it all just too disgusting. But, I suppose it was all part of the Soho tapestry of life.

At one time Ade put on a lesbian vibrator peep show with two girls, which made a fortune until the police closed it down. The money was so brilliant that the girls actually paid Ade a fee to let them work there. He charged about £50 and he was never short of takers for the shifts. It was a thriving business and was busy from the second it opened to the very last second of closing.

It was totally against the law. The police used to raid the peep shows all the time, going in with hammers and smashing the boxes to pieces and arresting anyone found in there.

After the police raided one set-up, Ade would charge around Soho and get a bunch of lads together and the peep show would be back up and running within an hour of the raid.

It was crazy to watch.
The peep show boxes were only made out of thick chipboard and they always had some on stand-by.
It was another game between club owners, council and police.

It was around this time when one of the big Maltese players in the West End opened a tiny club in one of the many Soho backstreets. He came past Greens Court one day. He had heard of my reputation as a very strong bar person and that I was very trustworthy and offered me a job. He wanted me to run the club for him. I would get a good percentage of any money taken and I would be able to choose my own staff.

It was a risk, leaving a successful club and giving all my shifts up but had to be worth a go. One of the door girls at Greens Court was a big polish girl called Clara. She was very good on the door and would work night and day to send money home for her child back in Poland. She was also a big gambler on the horses so she loved money. She was my first staff member.

Maggie said she would help me out. One of the Maltese, a little guy called Gigante was to do the bar with me. He was a big heroin user and I wasn't too happy about this choice but he was a personal friend of the owner.

The club opened and once it started going well girls would turn up for shifts. It began to get a bit of a reputation as a hard club, meaning we didn't take any prisoners as far as the punters were concerned. They didn't get out until they had paid and were sometimes roughed up if they argued.
However, we made money, so we didn't really care.

With the club being a bit out of the way, off the main drag, we didn't get as many punters, so we had to work really hard with the ones we did get. Many times I can remember all hell kicking off in the club and we would have to literally fight with the punter to get them to pay. It was very lively sometimes, but none of us seemed to have any fear factor, probably because nearly all the girls and men who worked the clubs were high on something; heroin, cocaine or speed.

People used a variety of drugs in those days but crack still wasn't a widely popular drug, even though we all sometimes dabbled at washing the cocaine in test tubes. Then, no-one knew it as crack, it was just known as 'clean coke'.

Once we gained a reputation we got a lot of police visits. Punters paid up most of the time without any problem. On the rare occasion that they brought the police back, it was a good tactic just to be pleasant to them and to give the money straight back. Even though a while earlier we had been shouting and screaming at them, pushing and threatening all sorts of things to make them pay. It saved us getting arrested for robbery

In other clubs, bar staff would try and argue with the police and say the punter had been sat down with a hostess and that he had also offered to buy the drinks. This always fell on deaf ears. There was also a good chance of being charged with anything from deception to robbery to demanding money with menaces or even blackmail and kidnapping! Some of these charges carried a prison sentence of up to ten years. It just wasn't worth arguing.
The law won every time.

The police and the council hated everything about us. We were scumbags, robbing innocent tourists of lots of money they would otherwise spend locally, and legally. They hated the fact that we had found loop-holes in the law and we were getting away with robbery right under their very noses.

I can still remember different punters from the years I worked in Soho.
I had some good ones and some that were not so good.

The Japanese were always everyone's favourite. They had a never ending supply of money it seemed and mostly just paid, they very rarely came back with the police. We also used to get the 'I want to take you shopping,' ones who were a real treat. They always had bags of money and would take us on a quick trip down Oxford Street. It didn't happen very often but was nice when it did.

Some were a bit strange but I sat with them anyway, money was money. They could have had two heads and we would have still sat there talking rubbish with them for as long as they were paying for it.

One couple came in, a man and a woman, nice enough but a little odd. They bought a couple of cocktails for me and paid the bill with no problem.
Then, much to my surprise they asked if they could do the show for me and the rest of the staff. At first I thought they were joking, but quickly realised this was what they had wanted to do since they came in. They had only bought me drinks out of politeness. I didn't know what to say and asked the barmaid what I should do.

'Why not?' She shrugged.

I knew if the police appeared they could close us down for something like this. I closed the top door so no-one could come in and the couple, very excited performed on the bed. I couldn't watch and disappeared into the toilet while they got on with it. They had full sex on the bed in front of the other staff, finished the show and then got dressed.

The woman thanked us and said she had longed to come into a sex club and do a show. It had been a fantasy of hers for years. Her partner just smiled and they both left looking very pleased with themselves. Things like that didn't happen everyday, but you just never know what sexual preferences people have. It's so strange what turns some people on

# Going Dutch

With the bad publicity from the police and the council wanting to close the clip joints down, the clubs went through a quiet period. Everyone seemed to be moaning about having no money or no prospect of things improving. Shifts were cut and the police were arresting as many people connected to the clubs as they could. They loved it when a punter approached them and muttered the words 'I've just been robbed in one of those clubs.'

I had given up running the club, Peter Street after about six months or so. I had come to dislike the owner, Carlos. He was too flash, up his own arse and thought everyone owed him a living.

But, it was the barman I had taken an instant dislike to, Gigante, who was the main cause of my leaving there. My first instinct about him had been right. He was a smack-head and it was he who insisted we took every punter to the cleaners. We had to virtually strip them to make sure they had no money hidden on them. His lust for money to feed his habit was so great.

We had the police being called every five minutes and if I carried on working there I saw myself in Holloway soon. It was safer with all the increased police activity, to go and work for someone else rather than run a club myself and so I left.

It was a dodgy time to be working anywhere in that environment, there was a high chance of being arrested. Most people were looking for an alternative way to earn money, something else other than club work. A lot more clippers were on the streets and the peep-show girls were paying up to £200 just to work a shift. Little Ade was making a fortune.

I was still taking heroin in large quantities. I had a £100 a day habit by that point and I was not earning the money I had become used to picking up.
I had to look for an alternative means of making money. I asked Little Ade if he had anything going. He said he had a mate who was offering an 'all expenses paid' weekend trip to Amsterdam. It was smuggling porno films into the UK from Holland. He made a fortune from each reel.

I had not been to Amsterdam before, I hadn't driven abroad either. With that in mind it sounded like quite an exciting adventure. I would speak to Don about it first but knew he would agree. I would be up for it if Don said yes.

In those days he was so laid back he would agree to virtually anything, but if he did have any concerns, an all expenses paid weekend in Amsterdam would probably sway him.

I had no work and called on Maggie who was no better off than I was; we were both short of money, so went clipping together. It was more of a risk during the day time. There was much more chance of being caught by the police or of a punter you had just ripped off, finding you.

We were lucky and found a Japanese man straight away who was very interested in Maggie. We said Maggie was interested in him and she told him what she would like to do to him, she promised him the earth and his excitement was very evident. It was so easy when the punter was so interested and a bonus when they didn't speak very good English. We got £300 off him in exchange for a key, pointed out the block where he should go and let himself in and then disappeared; leaving him to discover he had been well and truly clipped.
It was all so easy.

We went to The Intrepid Fox, not only was it a great pub, but also, we could hide upstairs and use the all round windows to make sure the coast was clear before gong back on the hunt for our next punter. We hoped the Japanese man had cut his losses and gone away by the time we had finished our drinks. If, by any chance, he was still around and we were unlucky enough to bump into him, we would say that the police had spotted us, and we had been forced to lie low for a while. Of course, we were worried he may have been arrested in a red light area and had been looking for him to warn him.
It worked every time.

We would arrange a meeting at a different door with yet another key and of course the same thing would happen again. The second time we would call it a day as the victim would catch on then and hang around on the off-chance they would see us and get their money back.
It was a very dangerous game of cat and mouse.

Looking back, I cannot believe the chances we took and the risks we all ran. Most of us did it in those days with little regard to the consequences.
I certainly wouldn't like to be working the streets now, what with all the knife and gun crime there is these days. Things were settled without weapons in the 80s. There didn't seem to be half as much violence as there is now. The club owners and girls had a genuine respect for each other.

I had been with Don for quite a while by this time and things were working out well. We enjoyed each others company and partied hard together. One afternoon, while I was working at Greens Court, I started to feel very unwell. I felt dizzy and sick and for once I didn't think it was down to drug abuse. The sick feeling just wouldn't go away and it got worse as the day wore on and even worse the next day.

I was still taking huge quantities of heroin, but I was convinced it wasn't down to the drugs, something was wrong. I shared my concerns with one of the girls at work and straight away she asked me if I could be pregnant.

I was shocked. It had never crossed my mind that I could be having a baby. I had never even considered the idea of having children. My whole life revolved around work, partying and drugs.
Bringing a child into that world was unthinkable.

One of the girls went and got me a pregnancy testing kit from the chemist. First thing the next morning I disappeared into the bathroom and used it.

Positive.

For at least an hour I sat just staring at the dreaded line.
Finally, I went to work but my mind just wasn't on the job.
All I could think about was the life that was growing inside me and how much harm I was doing the baby by taking so many drugs.

The shift went very slowly. Don was meeting me from work with Maggie's brother; we had arranged to go for a meal that evening.
When my shift finished the usual crowd turned up at The Fox and we all went out. Don soon guessed something was wrong and kept asking me what the matter was. I just shook my head.
Finally I admitted I was pregnant.
He stared at me in disbelief.

'No!' he said. 'It can't happen!'

He said he had two children already with his ex-wife and just didn't want any more. I was upset, really upset. He had not even considered what I might want. Then he brought the drugs into the equation.
How I could even consider bringing a child into the world while I was addicted to heroin?

He then said something that shook me to the core. He gave me an ultimatum. I would have to get rid of the baby or our relationship was over.
It was harsh and the last thing I expected. I couldn't finish my meal; I made my excuses and left the restaurant getting a taxi on my own.
I was upset, emotional and shocked.
How he could make me choose like that?

I don't know what time he eventually arrived home as I had cried myself to sleep.

The next day we didn't speak to each other. I went into work and met up with Rene. We sat down and talked. I didn't want to get rid of my baby I told her. I hadn't wanted one in the first place, but now it was growing inside me it was a different.

It was a life.
It was my child.

Rene didn't agree with me and also mentioned the drugs and my lifestyle. How the hell could I bring a child into that world? We were both emotional, crying and hugging each other.

The pain was incredible.
Everybody was against me.
For the first time in my life, I was helpless.
It was a dreadful feeling.

When I got home Don was already there. He smiled at me saying he totally understood how I was feeling but that we couldn't possibly have a child, not with the way we lived our lives.

If I had a baby it would be addicted to heroin from the start. He was blaming me for being a junkie. Then he dropped the bombshell. He had booked me into a clinic called Marie Stopes to have an abortion. It was a private and expensive place. I was, he informed me, booked in for the next morning.

I don't think I slept that night. The night seemed to last forever. In the morning a taxi was outside waiting for us. We didn't speak on the way. When we got there, the place was so white and clean. It had a strange odour that if I close my eyes now I can still smell. The nurse who I saw was very nice, putting her arm round me like she understood what I was going through.

I wanted to keep my baby.
No-one could understand my pain.
I knew Don was right.

They dressed me in what looked like a sheet. I was in an almost trance like state when the doctor arrived, a Chinese man.

Suddenly I was going into theatre.

In my head I changed my mind and screamed for them to stop.
I wanted my baby!
I stayed silent and they took it from me.

Afterwards, I hurt so much inside. The mental pain was unbearable. I worked as many shifts as I could and took as much heroin as I could possibly take. Don and I stayed with each other. He told me he loved me more than anything in the world, but something in my love for him had been damaged, something had been lost.

Now, I was on a path of self-destruction. No-one could stop me, drugs and alcohol eased my pain. Don booked me a holiday to Tenerife hoping it would help my emotional state. It would take more than a few days in the sun to get rid of this pain.

There were years of torturous 'what ifs?' ahead of me.

My drug problem had spiralled. I was sacked from Greens Court for being unreliable so I went back to work in the strip clubs and the clip joints run by the black owners. The money was always better but the risks higher.
They were so violent towards punters who disputed their bills.

With all this in mind, I finally decided that I would take Ade up on his Amsterdam offer. Ade arranged that Don and I would meet the Maltese man at his flat and discuss the business trip.
Guze was pleasant enough and told us that he would hire us a new car for the trip, the reels were to be placed in the door panels so it had to be a Ford, because the door panels came off very easily.

We were to go to a hotel near Amsterdam railway station where our Dutch contact would meet up with us and give us the reels to bring back. Guze said the risks we were taking were not huge. If we got caught, all that would happen was that our house would be raided and we would be questioned. He would send his solicitor straight to us at no charge, and pay for any legal expenses incurred. He assured us that as it would be our first offence we'd just get a slap on the wrist and that would be the end of it all. The money would be good and we had a free weekend away to enjoy.

It all sounded so good and so easy. It all seemed really exciting. Don had to drive as I hadn't passed my driving test at that time, even though I drove, illegally, all the time at home. We set off from London. It was icy cold when we booked into the hotel but we went out straight away to explore 'The Dam'.

It was a very busy place with sex advertised everywhere. There were adverts for shows, ladies in doorways and windows. It was so very different to Soho, much more exciting. I was like a child in a sweet shop not knowing what to look at first or where to go in and explore.

We went to look at a live show. I was half expecting it to be like our 'live shows' but I was surprised. There was a round stage with seating all around it. A barmaid offered us a drink. Straight away I asked her how much the drinks were. I expected silly prices like we charged back home. She looked at me as if I was a bit strange. Here it was completely different. The drinks were alcoholic and the prices were the standard prices charged everywhere else in Amsterdam.

The show started and a man came out onto the stage followed by a woman and they began their performance. They danced for a while and then she gave him a blow job.

This definitely wasn't Soho, this was all for real. They moved around the stage in various positions so that everyone in the audience could see when he penetrated her. It was all very sexy and a real turn on. Don was very aroused so I performed my own act on him. When we had finished the whole audience applauded.

Wow! What a place Amsterdam was.

I fell in love with The Dam straight away. We spent the rest of the night in the many cafés which were dotted about, smoking weed from the menus that they provided. There were so many different types of weed to choose from.
The next day we just chilled out waiting for the Dutch contact to show up. When he did he showed us how to pack the reels into the car doors so we soon got things packed away and went off to enjoy the rest of our stay.

We went to another live show. This time it was girls doing different acts. The first one was a young Chinese girl with a collection of various vibrators.
She got the audience to insert the vibrators into her while she danced around the stage. They couldn't wait to get in on it.

The second act was a girl dressed in a tiny little tennis skirt and no knickers. She danced around teasing all the men and then produced a tennis racket from behind the stage and sat on the end of it.
It stuck out of her as she stood up sending the men wild.

When she finished all the lights went out and some strange music started. I told Don to keep his hand on his wallet, again I was thinking about how it was in Soho. If the lights went out there, there would be a good chance your money would disappear.

A girl came out dressed in a sequined bikini. She was stunning. She danced for a while then produced some candles. She lit the candles and performed a very sexy dance, holding the candles so they were dripping hot wax onto her body; all over her body. Hot wax dripped onto her nipples and anywhere else you could think of. Finally she put a candle so far inside her that just the flame was showing. Then she performed some acrobatics to show the candle still alight. It was an amazing show and I found it a real turn-on. We stayed for a couple of drinks after the show and the candle girl came over to us to ask if we had enjoyed her show. She told us that she worked in one of the windows at weekends normally and wanted us to do business with her. Would we be interested in a threesome?
We laughed at this and politely refused her kind offer. I had enjoyed the show, but that was as far as it went.

As we were about to leave, the strange music started again and another girl appeared on the stage. She asked for members of the audience to go onto the stage and grabbed at Don's hand but he shook his head to decline. Eventually she got a very odd mixture of six men up there. It amused me to see how worried a couple of them looked.

She got them to lie down on the stage and produced a banana which she inserted into her, and then she crouched over the men with it sticking out and invited them to take a bite of it.
A couple of the men refused, I don't blame them.

The last act of the performance was called the 'Ping-pong Show'. The lights went down and Japanese music was piped into the room. A young girl came out in a kimono and bowed to the audience. She looked as if she was about to do martial arts.

She removed her dress, and danced around sexily for a few minutes which the punters enjoyed. Then, she produced three ping-pong balls which she placed inside herself. She danced some more and then suddenly bent over and opened her very long legs in front of the waiting men and popped the balls out one after the other.
It was quite an amazing sight.
All the people watching were enthralled at this and as a woman I was amazed. How did she do it!

We moved on to a nearby café and chose from the extensive cannabis menu. It was nearly time to leave this extraordinary place and as I sat smoking I thought to myself that I could quite easily live here, but probably would be dead within six months.

The next morning we got our stuff together and said goodbye to Amsterdam and headed back to England with the reels of porn in the door cavities.
We boarded the ferry without a problem.

I knew the chances of being caught were slight and, Guze had assured us that if we were it would merely be a slap on the wrist. But I still couldn't help feeling nervous, nervous and excited at the same time.

When we arrived back in England the adrenaline really started flowing. As we drove off the ferry we could see some customs officers watching the procession of cars leaving the ferry.

I was absolutely convinced they were looking for us. As we got nearer they seemed to be looking straight at us. Suddenly as we got right up to them one of them started to wave us over.

Oh no! I thought to myself panicking, but Don carried on driving at a steady pace.

'What are you doing Don?' I asked, 'Won't they chase us?'

Don just laughed, 'Look behind you' he said.

I turned round and saw that they hadn't been waving at us at all! Of course! If they had meant for us pull over they wouldn't have waited until we were on top of them. I was so relieved. It was all over! We had done it!

It was after the trip I decided I would try to get off heroin. Don was helping me. I went to the doctors and they prescribed methadone. I knew it wasn't going to be an easy journey. The sickness and the constant pains in my legs were unbearable.

The club at Greens Court took me back on and I was working my shifts. I was doing well and I was made bar manager. Because I was coming off the heroin my weight started to increase. Punters liked big girls but I wasn't interested, I preferred working the bar. For one I didn't have to wear any revealing clothing. The girls ribbed me a bit about the weight I was putting on, but I didn't mind.
Every pound gained was a small victory over heroin.

But, heroin was still a large shadow lurking in the background and I would suffer a lapse every now and again which caused huge rows between Don and me. It wasn't easy, but lapses aside, I was determined to shake my dependence of the drug.

Heroin controls you; it is constantly there in the back of your mind. Just one more hit, and that will be my last. I imagine its something all junkies say to themselves. Even after all these years the temptation is still always there.

The big police clampdown and council campaign against the clubs had run out of steam and things in the West End started to get back to normal.
For the time being anyway, punters were flooding back into the area and offering easy targets for us.

After a couple of weeks, Little Ade called round to ask us if we would do another porn run to Amsterdam for Guze.
We were alright for money now and we didn't really have to go but I fancied a free weekend in Amsterdam again.

I told Ade I would ask Don and get back to him. When I asked Don he said yes straight away, but we agreed that this would be the last trip.

Famous last words!

We were going at the weekend and Don had organised a hire car. There was a problem with it; we couldn't get the Ford.

That should have served as a warning.

We arrived in The Dam, found our hotel and met up with the contact. He struggled to get the door panels off to put the reels in. With Don's help the panels finally came off. The reels went inside, but then they had a real struggle getting the door panels back on. When they had finished it was obvious that the panels had been tampered with.

We should've called it off there and then but it had been so easy last time we weren't that worried. We spent the rest of our time in Amsterdam touring the cannabis cafés. This trip didn't feel as glamorous or exciting as the first one.

I left Don in one coffee shop to phone home and managed to score some heroin from a Moroccan at the same time. I took it straight away and hoped Don wouldn't notice. When I returned, he realised as soon as he saw me and we had a blazing row; returning to the hotel not talking and very unhappy.

The heroin I had bought had been cut with something other than the usual glucose. It made me very ill and my stomach was in pieces. I spent the rest of the weekend in bed in the hotel.

The morning we returned to the UK was freezing and we left early in case the roads were bad. As I waited at the front of the hotel for Don to get the car, two young Africans approached me. I didn't know what they wanted at first.
Suddenly they attacked me, grabbing at my bag.

Working in the Soho clubs for years had taught me how to look after myself. I fought back, kicking and clawing at them. Our passports, money and keys were in my bag and they wouldn't get it without the fight of their lives.

After what seemed like ages, they took off with nothing. I was really shaken; no-one had come to my aid. The man on the hotel reception had even locked the door while I was fighting them off. Angrily I went in and asked him why he had locked me out. He just grunted that people like that always carried knives and were prepared to use them. He didn't want them getting into the hotel and starting on him. He was so scared and I realised that I had been very lucky.

Don pulled up in the car. He was still very angry that after all the hard work we had been doing to keep me off the heroin, I had given in to temptation, and we still weren't speaking properly yet. He was shocked when I told him how I had just fought the two men off but as we made our way to the port at Rotterdam we still said very little to each other.

We sped through the winter landscape and I relaxed more as the heater in the car warmed me up. I was in a world of my own as I looked out of the window. We passed through a few Dutch villages with people ice-skating on little ponds. It was very idyllic and pretty.

Again we boarded the ferry with no problems. As we passed through the English customs at the other end, I started to feel really sick. I got a very bad feeling about it all.

Sure enough, as we went through the checkpoints, a customs officer beckoned to us to pull over. Don steered the car to the place he pointed us to.
The customs officer checked the boot, thanked us and said we could drive on. Then, as Don got back in the car and slammed the door, one of the door panels fell off and he couldn't shut the door properly. The customs man saw there was a problem and opened the door to see if he could help.

To his obvious delight, he discovered the reels neatly tucked away plus a few that had fallen out onto the car floor. I felt my heart skip a beat as he stared at us accusingly.

He ordered us out of the car and fired questions at us.
We said nothing and were then taken into a building and processed.
They split us up and I was held in a small room until I was eventually interviewed. The questions seemed to go on for ever. Two customs officers interviewed me doing the good cop/bad cop routine, Mr Nice and Mr Nasty, blowing hot and cold to try and get answers out of me.

Neither of us would speak and this led them to believe we must be carrying drugs as well as porn. They kept us for thirty-six hours and told us they were entitled to hold us for another seventy-two. If they still didn't get any answers then, they would hand us over to the police.

If I needed the toilet I had to go in a cubicle with only half a door and a conveyer belt at the side so they could check if drugs had been swallowed and passed. I knew we didn't have any drugs and the thought that they had to root through my shit for nothing cheered me up no end.

I was questioned for what seemed like every waking hour and continually strip-searched. The searches were followed by cold showers while the officers looked on making sarcastic comments.

Don said later they had done the same thing to him, making lewd comments about his manhood. It got them nowhere so they upped the ante and tried intimidating us.

The interviews turned into interrogations.

They put us both into a room where they told us to strip off and we were made to stand in a corner of the room completely naked. Someone held my arms from behind and a customs officer blocked Don's nose and mouth with the palm of their hand. Another one twisted his testicles.
We still said nothing.

Eventually they gave up and transferred us to a near-by police station in Felixstowe where they woke us up every hour with more questions.
They told us they knew exactly where we lived, that they knew Don was from Northern Ireland and had children. They told him he wouldn't see his kids for years unless we gave them information. Don was close to cracking when they said that, but we kept it together and told them nothing.

The policeman looking after us informed us that they had raided our flat and found drugs. At that time we had a five foot long snake. Our drugs were in the snake's cage. We often kept drugs in there as not many people would put their hands in to take it.

The police asked if it was poisonous, I refused to tell them and they said they would have to call London Zoo in to deal with it. I found that really funny and laughed when they said it, which annoyed them even more.

They said that we would be able to go shortly as they had raided several places in Soho successfully and had got who they wanted. We hadn't acknowledged the Soho connection but they knew where we worked and who our associates were.

The solicitor that we had been promised never appeared and we soon realised things were not how they seemed and the promise of help was a lie. We were constantly told that we were looking at up to nine years in prison if they had enough evidence and they had more than enough they informed us.

Eventually they released us; they said we would be black-listed by car hire companies and not to leave the country as the case would be going to court. They dropped us at the nearest railway station and eventually, we got home.

After the stressful hours locked up in Felixstowe, we slept for ages.
We awoke to someone banging on the door. It was Ade seeing if we were alright. We told him everything that had happened and he said not to worry about it, they hadn't got anything apart from the reels. We saw on the news that raids had taken place. Some of the Maltese had been arrested and in particular a huge quantity of porn had been seized from a big house in South London and a major porn ring busted.

I went into Soho the next day for my normal shift at Greens Court. No-one knew what I had been up to. I just said I had been at home for the weekend.

It was best kept quiet. Everyone got suspicious if anyone got arrested, people would ask 'will they tell all, or will they keep quiet?'

The shift started well with a nice European man in first, who really liked the ladies, he asked for all three on duty to join him for drinks. As usual he wanted far more than what was on offer. For a small fee, we guided him upstairs to the 'models' who plied their trade above the club. We said he was more than welcome to come back down to the club to see our show when he had finished with the models, but knew he wouldn't come back once he had done what he needed to.

The buzzer did go again but it was Ade. He came down to say that Guze, the Maltese man we had done the Amsterdam runs for, wanted to meet us. He needed to know what had gone wrong. I didn't have a problem with this and told Don what Ade had said. Don, being from Northern Ireland, was suspicious of everyone and said he would only meet him in a public place. We met at The Globe, a well known pub on Baker Street, a very public place lessening the risk of us being attacked or worse.

It was a wet, miserable day but the man greeted us and the conversation started off quite pleasantly. But as we discussed what had happened, the accusations started flying and he demanded to know exactly what we had told the police and customs. Until this point Don had been quite calm, as had I.

We told him the truth; all we had told them were our names and had refused to say anything else, even though we had been given the 'special treatment'. He didn't believe us and a very heated argument started. In the end he warned us never to go into the West End again. He could make life very difficult for us. He had friends and family in Ireland and Don's family could be 'spoken to'.

We decided to stay away from the West End. We were scared, we both knew what the Maltese were capable of and for a good few weeks we were looking over our shoulders for Maltese types, remembering the beating Scouse Mike had received from Maltese with bike chains. We also believed that the police were following us to find other Maltese they desperately wanted to arrest.

Don's nerves were in tatters. If he had to leave the house for work he used his motorbike, it was the only way he felt safe. We also moved, to a friend's house on White Hart Lane in Tottenham. I took a 'straight job' for a despatch company for a short while.
Then, purely by chance, Don bumped into Dougie, my first proper Maltese friend. Dougie couldn't believe what had happened and told Don the Maltese in question was no-one and we should have no fear of him. Dougie and his friends did not like this man and he would have to go through him before he did anything to us. We were safe to return to the West End and Soho.

It was an easy decision to return to making good money for doing next to nothing. And, although I still looked over my shoulder a lot of the time, really, I knew I was more than safe.

One of the girls I worked with, Karen, was a heavy binge drinker, always getting into bother when she hit the vodka. We all tried our best to get her to go straight home after her shift, but more often than not she would go to the Red Lion and drink with the Maltese, then come back to the club and be a pain. If she couldn't find anyone else to argue with, she would sit and argue with herself. Sober, she had a heart of gold, would do anything for anyone and was a good friend.

Shirley, an old school East Ender and Karen's mum, used to do the bar sometimes in Greens Court. One day I went in for my shift. The club was still closed but no-one seemed to know why and the staff waited outside for a good hour until one of the bosses arrived. Shirley had passed away of natural causes during the night, totally unexpectedly and she had the keys to the club. We were all very sad about this news, not everybody liked Shirley but she had been a real character. I did worry for Karen though. She was very close to her mother and this certainly wouldn't help her drink problem. Sure enough, towards the end of the shift, Karen appeared. She was drinking neat vodka. Sarah, one of the other girls and I took her to a taxi and persuaded her to get in and I went with her to make sure she got home as she was in such a state.

Karen asked if I would help her to do food for the funeral. I knew there would be a lot of people there, Shirley was well thought of in Soho and the East End and the funeral was a big event, there were some famous faces there that you really wouldn't want to mess with. Karen kept herself together very well. .
The West End carried on as before. People were sad for a short while about the death of Shirley but nothing changed apart from Karen's drinking got a lot worse.

# Haft Na Floose

People in Soho would come and go and sometimes come back again but there was always the faithful few that never seemed to move on.
But now, Soho itself was beginning to change; the people visibly so. A lot more drugs were coming in. Heroin was becoming unfashionable, crack was taking a hold on people and the scene was much more violent. As drug habits changed so did the girls. Those on crack were much more desperate for money.

With heroin you could easily do a shift on a single bag. The high from crack rocks only lasted around twenty minutes, so crack addiction needed more frequent fixes than heroin and so needed more money to support it. When the crack was wearing off the buzz would disappear and another crack stone was needed while they were still on the shift. More risks were taken with the punters to get as much money out of them as was possible as soon as possible.

With more risks taken there were more frequent visits from the police trying to get people on their favourite robbery and blackmail charge. I could see what was going on around me at this time and as a result I became more careful.

My good friend Maggie had become involved with an Australian lad who had moved into the Soho area. He had found The Fox and started hanging around with our crowd. He loved his music and hoped to become a musician in London. He was alright, but like Maggie and me he liked his heroin too much to clean up his act and become successful.

She had only been seeing him for a few weeks when she disappeared. She had run off to get married, not telling any of us what she'd done until she floated back again onto the scene as if nothing had happened. Maggie was always quite impulsive.

While she was away, her ex-boyfriend, Jerry appeared back on the scene. He had been in prison but was sorting his life out, supposedly. He started coming into The Fox regularly, trying to hang out with our crowd by having a few beers with us. When Maggie got back we worked a shift at Greens Court together catching up with the news of Soho and what she had missed while she was away, including the arrival back on the scene of Jerry.

Don was meeting me after work in The Fox and when Maggie and I got there he was pacing the bar really stressed, looking out of the many windows of the pub onto the street. I asked him what was wrong and then noticed an untouched pint next to his. Don said he had been having a beer with Jerry and asked him if he could get him any weed, which had dried up in Soho of late. Jerry had offered to go and get him some from one of his friends. Don had handed him a crisp twenty pound note and off Jerry had gone, leaving his pint on the bar. .

As he relayed the story to Maggie and me, we both burst out laughing. Don didn't know Jerry very well; Maggie and I wouldn't have trusted him with ten pence. We asked Don what time Jerry had left. He had been gone for a couple of hours. It looked as if Jerry was back to his old self. Don was livid when the penny finally dropped, which amused me and Maggie even more.

Don decided he would go out and about in Soho and look for Jerry and hopefully get either his money back or the weed. Maggie and I looked at each other; both thinking that he had no chance of finding Jerry. Don disappeared out of the door. He searched Soho and asked various people if they had seen Jerry but nobody had. He was about to give up when he went to a Maltese drinking den above the peep show on Great Windmill Street.

When he got there, Don found out that Jerry apparently owed money everywhere. He met one of the Maltese called 'Mario'; a lot of the Maltese were called Mario. This Mario had been in prison with Jerry. Jerry was being released first with nowhere to go, so Mario said that if he paid the rent of his fully furnished flat, he could use it until he, himself got out.

Finally, Mario had been released and went straight to his flat, which was now emptied of all his belongings and on which no rent had been paid. He was as mad as hell with Jerry and after him as well. He said he'd join Don in the hunt for Jerry. Don got a little nervous as Mario then packed a gun into his jacket.
Suddenly his twenty pounds didn't seem so important.

Mario decided the best place to look for Jerry would be Kings Cross. If he was avoiding the West End he would go to the Cross, especially if he knew people were looking for him. Mario asked Don for a lift there and Don obliged even though he was beginning to wish he had never asked Mario anything.
This was getting far too serious.

They got to Kings Cross and asked around if anyone had seen Jerry. Someone said they had seen him score there about an hour previously. They asked another dealer by the Wimpy. He replied that he was only on the streets because he had been told Jerry was around; Jerry owed him a lot of money!

By this time Mario was at boiling point and they still hadn't found him.
All they had found were others that he had ripped off. Don decided enough was enough and told Mario it was hopeless and dropped him off back in Soho.
Mario promised Don he would find Jerry and deal with him.

Don came back to The Fox and told us why he had been gone so long. We had a couple more drinks then walked down Old Compton Street passing the market. As we went down one of the many back alleys, there, sprawled across a pile of bin bags was Jerry, lying there with the rest of the rubbish.

He was completely off his face but we could see he had also been badly beaten. We just carried on walking. I don't think it was Mario that had found him, as he appeared to be still alive. But he had obviously bumped into someone he had ripped off and got a bit of what he deserved.

We heard later, that when he had recovered from the beating he had bought some more gear and got stopped by the police with it on him. So off he went for another stay in prison. With the number of people that wanted a piece of him, this probably saved his life,

Things were moving on at a fast rate in Soho, the clubs were building up again and the number of punters was up. We had become friends with the model who worked above Greens Court and we used to send her quite a bit of business from punters who thought they would get a bit of something in the club. We charged them a small amount, maybe fifty pounds and then took them up to the model. The model would then charge them again for whatever they were after.

Everything was about how much you could get.

The model would call downstairs afterwards to thank us. Her name was Vicky and she was from Leeds. She was really nice. She paid a high rent to her Maltese landlord but made enough money to only have to work three times a week.

She told us stories of what punters liked to do. An Asian man who was a regular punter of hers waited upstairs until she had been with a black man and then asked her not to wash. He liked to go down on her straight after the black punter had left.

We all thought that was utterly disgusting but she said he paid her a lot extra for that particular service. She also used to have a business-man from the city that had a thing about being treated like a baby. He would turn up in a very expensive looking suit, probably straight from Savile Row, carrying a black leather bag.

The bag contained an adult sized rubber baby-gro complete with pink frills and a pair of frilly pink leather pants to match. He also had a big plastic dummy. He liked to be the baby for half an hour or so with Vicky telling him what a good boy he had been while changing his nappy. She would have to feed him with a baby spoon and he would wear a rubber bib. He didn't speak, just made baby gurgling noises.
When this all finished he would get back into his expensive suit and either go back to work or back to his wife. I don't know how Vicky kept a straight face with some of the mad requests that she had.

It was all so surreal. But everything has a price.

The models were always very busy. You would see punters darting up the stairs quickly so they wouldn't be noticed. Greens Court was in an alleyway and the model's punters would scuttle up, looking around and over their shoulders to make sure no one was watching.
Sometimes I would shout 'live show!' just as they were about to run up for the models, which annoyed them but amused me.

Times were definitely changing in Soho and I can honestly say not for the better. The heavier police presence pushed the vice and drugs underground, and people were getting more desperate for money.

It didn't seem to matter that the police were giving warnings out to punters to avoid the clubs. The club was still busy, maybe not as busy as we could've been but we were still making good money.

Towards the last part of my Soho days, a new breed of people seemed to be moving in. I got to know three new girls, Joanna, Sammy and Lucy. These three were young, sassy girls who had no scruples whatsoever. Money was god to them and they didn't care how they obtained it.

They were hard as nails.

One of them was the daughter of an old clipper. The other two were best friends who had come to Soho together to work. They liked to play hard and worked to make enough money to play as hard as they possibly could. Every night was a party night to them. They reminded me of myself when I had first moved into the West End. I did like the three of them; they were just like me only younger and fresher. All three of them were on either crack or coke.
The more money they earned the more they spent on drugs.

# Soho People

Soho has always been schizophrenic, with the pedestrian everyday thriving beside the erotic and exotic; a place of extremes.

The world I lived in evolved from Soho's own history of migratory and transient people getting by as best they can, with everything that can be sold having a price and multitudes of willing buyers.

The people of Soho, the girls, the boys and the punters were as many and varied as the history of Soho itself.

When I began work at Greens Court I met Antonia, a very tall Italian woman in her late twenties. We became friends and worked together there for a good few years. She was very popular with the punters; probably down to her long legs and the flair she had. She had a slim build with long dark hair. She didn't always get her words quite right which was amusing to the rest of our circle but she had an air of arrogance about her.

Antonia had a serious heroin problem but oddly, it never affected her work in Soho. It was very rare that she didn't turn up for her shift and was one of the most reliable of the staff. She did a lot of the shows and very rarely received any complaints.

Paul, her boyfriend, was a beggar. He went begging everyday while she worked to support his heroin habit as well as her own. He was a very unpleasant person; scruffy and dirty looking, a complete waste of space.
He often appeared at the club asking her for money and got angry if she had none for him.
He existed only for his next fix.

Antonia always seemed sad and often talked about going home, but never got the money together to return. I worked with her for six or seven years in all and I can't remember her ever going home once, not even for a holiday.
At the time we were earning anything from £100 to £400 a shift and most of us did double shifts - eleven to eleven.

She was one of many living life hand to mouth on amounts like this. She paid no

rent or mortgage as she lived in a squat in north London. She would only eat the odd yogurt or sweet thing; so food shopping wasn't high on her agenda.
All her money went on her and her boyfriend's heroin habits.

Toni often worked the door and had an instinct where punters were concerned, a real knack. She knew the ones with money and being Italian she tempted a fair few rich Italians into the club. They always spent well.
She was clever; when she spoke to them in Italian my guess is that she got them to ask for her to come down and sit with them and someone else had to cover the door.

To be fair, she always invited the hostess whose turn it was to greet that customer, to join them for a drink. That meant if the punter paid, Toni kept the door money and also received a cut of the bill. We all learnt this trick when doing the door and most of us told punters that we could leave the door and join them for the very sexy show and have some private time with them. Antonia was a good all rounder and worked the West End well.

We worked alongside a girl from London, tall with mousey, shoulder length hair, Karen. She had had a rough upbringing and lived in East London with her Maltese husband and two little boys.

Her mum, Shirley, also worked in the club bar, she was very drawn and haggard. She had worked the clubs in the era of the 1950s East End gangsters the Krays. She was very proud of the fact and told us all the stories from those days if we sat down during a quiet shift. She and Karen, both characters, would keep us amused for hours. There was never any mention of Karen's father, but I believe he had worked alongside the Kray twins. Karen and I spent a lot of time with each other, working a lot of shifts together. She had a big drink problem, drinking neat vodka from the minute she got up, all the way through the day.

On many occasions she would be too drunk to work but when she did work she was a very good hostess. She was probably not the best looking girl in the West End but still managed to get the punters to buy her drinks. Karen and I became competitive on who would make the most money and argued about who did the best show. That's how she was, she was very competitive, and everything was a game to her. Karen's shows were something else when she was drunk; she revealed more than she should have done quite often.

Karen had worked Soho since she was 14 and had drunk heavily the whole time. Soho was her whole life, maybe because she had got married very young and to a much older man. Her husband was quiet and never came down to Soho unless he was meeting with his Maltese friends for a drink.
We stayed friends for many years and shared a lot of laughs together.

Clara was Polish. She spoke in broken English that was very amusing to hear but even without her odd English she kept us laughing; a naturally funny girl.
We all thought she was more into women than men until she started seeing a Frenchman she met in a club. He was really strange. He would watch over her as she worked on the door, almost like a stalker. We didn't know it at the time but she was pregnant with his child.

One shift she asked for some time off to visit her mother in Poland. I don't know if it was that we were all so stoned in those days but nobody clocked on that she was about to drop and she'd said nothing to anybody about being pregnant

She went to Poland, had the baby then returned to England on her own, leaving the child with her mother. When she got back, her French boyfriend went mental, really angry that she had not brought his baby back with her. He made her life a misery from then on, never leaving her alone.

Clara carried on working in Soho like nothing had happened and sent money home all the time for her daughter. Occasionally she would show us pictures of her that her mother sent. Other than that she never really mentioned her little girl at all.

Another girl I got to know quite well was Annie from Leeds. A strange looking woman with a mass of hair going into dreadlocks, about 5'3 and stocky; usually wearing short skirts and strange tights. I happened, one day to wander into a club she was in; she had been drinking and was a bit unstable.

Annie had been in the Soho area since she was thirteen as a hostess and working the streets as a prostitute. Her sister who worked the doors was called Mad Esther. She was tall and slim, the complete opposite to Annie. It was bizarre to see them together.

Annie was actually quite a good hostess, despite the mess she looked, but she would sleep with anyone if they said they liked her. Years of abuse as a child had given her very low self-esteem.

Soon after we met, Annie invited me to her sister's for tea. She seemed so lonely, I didn't really want to go but I didn't want to upset her so I said that I would. A woman opened Esther's door to us in full make up and heels. I said hello but Annie seemed really annoyed with her. Annie and I chatted a while and the woman went upstairs. After a short while Annie said she wanted the loo and went upstairs too.

And then I heard her yelling angrily. I didn't know what to do and stayed where I was until she ran back downstairs shouting:

'Look at him! Can you believe this? You must tell Esther!'

I was confused, I hardly knew Annie, and hadn't met Esther yet.
I wondered what I had let myself in for.

Following Annie down the stairs was a man with a wig wearing ladies underwear, I recognised him as the 'lady' that had answered the door.

It was Esther's boyfriend. We had caught him dressing up in her clothes. I nearly died with embarrassment and didn't know what to say or do. Never in my life had I seen anything like this.

We soon left the house. Annie insisted that we went straight back down to Soho to tell Esther all about it. Esther was working on the door of Ambience and Annie ran up to her shouting that her boyfriend was a freak and a poof and that we had caught him wearing her clothes. I didn't know where to look.

Mad Esther asked me calmly,

'Is this true?'

This was the first time I had met Mad Esther. I told her that when we had got to the house, I had thought her boyfriend was her. She looked away and carried on calling punters in, as if nothing had happened.
I believe she stayed with him, which I found strange.

After a couple of years, Annie fell pregnant by one of the club owners; a man in his 50s. We were all really concerned about this as Annie couldn't even look after herself let alone a child. She carried on drinking and working right up until she gave birth to a little girl.
The club owner provided for the child and Annie went back to work leaving the baby with a woman she knew. This woman ended up adopting the little girl and Annie was allowed visits.
In the end, like many others Annie got hooked on crack and would turn tricks with anyone who would pay her.

In Soho, there were Maltese owned illegal drinking dens. They were in Great Windmill Street above some of the black owned clubs. They were mainly used for gambling and drinking after hours. A lot of the club girls would use them to go and score drugs. Some of the Maltese used to sell drugs and some of the black men did too.

Towards the end of my time in Soho, as crack was becoming more prevalent, some of the girls would be quiet desperate for the drug and money wasn't as readily available as it had been.

One night, I was sitting in one of the drinking dens having a quiet drink with one of the girls after a long shift. Annie came into the club looking to score some crack, without any money. She offered to give one of the dealers a blow job in return for some crack.

He refused her offer; she wasn't the best looking girl in the world. He sat there laughing with some of the guys who were in there. Another man had a mongrel called 'Commando' because it was so scared of anybody and anything that it crawled along on its belly most of the time. He said if she was that desperate she could give the dog a blow job. To which she readily replied, 'ok!'

She got on all fours and gave the dog a blow job. The dog was obviously enjoying it, as were the men inside the club who were laughing and joking as this desperate drug addict shed her last ounce of self respect and performed a sex act on a dog.

This was a real shame, as until then Annie had stayed clear of the drug scene. But she ended up prostituting herself again. I believe the early years of abuse and losing her child, brought her to a point of no return.

Melissa was Italian and in her 40's when I first met her and always worked the doors. She came from a rich background and was quite snooty. She was married to a Japanese man and they had one child. Melissa was very over the top, wearing high platform shoes and way out clothes but was always dressed immaculately, with full makeup. She was quite short with big brown hair or sometimes she would wear a wig, whichever took her fancy. She was a real character, making us laugh all the time and we all loved her.

She used to tell such lies on the door, telling punters anything to get them inside. When the irate punters came back up from the club she would hide from them in the shop next door. It was so comical. If the punter was angry enough to wait and was there when she reappeared she would scream as if they were going to kill her as soon as she saw them. This worked very well and more often than not, they ran away.

Melissa's lies could get us into some real scrapes though. One day she sent two Arabs downstairs to us telling them they would get full sex after the show. We took a lot of money off them and then they just sat there, waiting. We asked them what they were waiting for as they had seen the show.

'We want our sex time now,' said one of them.

Now we were worried. I ran up to Melissa and she told me it was the only way she could get them in. So, we had two angry Arabs wanting to get their bits out and we never did anything even close to touching, let alone full sex.
And, of course, Melissa disappeared.

So, we did the next best thing and took them to the real prostitutes in the flats above the clubs. We had to give them some of the bill for the Arabs needs and lost quite a bit of commission, but the punters were happy, the police weren't called and the club stayed in one piece. This happened quite frequently with Melissa but we always had a laugh about it afterwards.

Melissa made a lot of money on the door, making the prices up if she thought the punter had a lot of money. Her husband thought she was a secretary in the City and never questioned where she was.

She never got into drugs and didn't drink either, but she was always going on about losing weight. At this time, a close friend and I were dealing in speed as a little side-line, selling it round the clubs we knew. We suggested that she tried some. Eventually she said she would try it. We said we would get it for her. Knowing that she hadn't got a clue about drugs, we crunched a couple of paracetamols up and wrapped the powder in cling film.
We then charged her £10 a wrap.

Melissa was very pleased with her new slimming drug and this little deal carried on for a good few years. Sometimes we would tell her how slim and beautiful she looked.

Melissa worked the doors in quite a few clubs including Ambience, Greens Court, Erotica, Maximillian's and the Pink Pussycat. She was very good on the doors, even with all the lies. As long as everyone told her how beautiful she looked we had a good shift.

I am not proud of what we did, but selling relatively harmless substances as hard drugs wasn't an unusual thing in Soho. I'm sure we weren't the only ones doing it. Melissa always seemed grateful and it didn't do her any harm.

Towards the end of my days in Soho Melissa started getting greedy. The Greens Court door was next to a door which led to prostitutes flats. The punters visiting the prostitutes would slide into the doorway. Sly Melissa charged them to go upstairs, even though the prostitutes were nothing to do with the club. They paid very high rent to a landlord for the room and the rest was their money.

One particular day, we heard a right shouting match going on upstairs.
We ran up to see if Melissa was alright and found one of the prostitutes holding Melissa by the hair had and landing punches and kicks wherever she could with Melissa screaming for help.

We all dived in and got the prostitute to let go. Then we found out exactly what Melissa had been up to. Melissa ran off and we didn't see her again for nearly two weeks, then she reappeared like nothing had happened.

She got a warning from Cass and apologised to the prostitutes. To be honest, we didn't care as she was so good on the door, and if she wanted would have let her get away with it again.

Black Beryl was a funny girl. She reminded us all of the little black woman in the Police Academy films with the sweet 'Minnie Mouse' voice; until somebody annoyed her, then she turned into a screeching banshee.

'Bee' as we knew her could write a book of excuses for being late, which she always was.

The best I ever heard was her glass eye, that often used to fall out, but only ever in the mornings. It was searching for it that made her late and of course, she would say it was harder for her because she only had the one good eye to look for it with.

She got on the only bus in London that lost its way. And all the other buses broke down as soon as she set foot on them.

If she had come to work on the underground, there was always a dramatic story about how the tube had been held up. Suicidal maniacs always chose her train to throw themselves under.

Beryl wasn't her real name, she never told anyone what her real name was, or her age. Not that it mattered but we thought it strange. The men she was with always seemed a lot younger than she was.

We all loved working with her but she could be sly and try to nick the good punters off you swearing that it was her turn, not yours. We were wise to her little tricks and took it with a pinch of salt. She was harmless and really, I think we all thought of her as a sort of mother figure.

Kathy was from Dublin and in her early 20s, quite small in stature. She was a heroin addict who injected, and had run away from her life and very strict Catholic parents in Dublin to England.

Her brother, Paddy came to London to look for her, to 'save' her.
She was really into punk music and he found her in the Intrepid Fox.
He was very glad to see her and it was obvious he cared about her very much.

Paddy was your average Irish farmer and a little lost in the big city.
He stayed with us for about 3 weeks, trying to persuade her to return home. He eventually gave up and returned to Ireland.
When he left, her drug taking spiralled out of control.

She met a car-thief, another Dubliner called Sean who was not a nice character at all. He was a big supporter of the IRA and wouldn't think twice about robbing an old lady. He had no morals whatsoever and used to knock Kathy about.

Don and I were living in Willesden at the time and we had a communal pay-phone in the entrance hall to the house in which we rented a flat. She would often ring us to pick her up as Sean had beaten her up. These phone calls became more and more frequent as their relationship deteriorated.

One night, we were in bed and we heard the phone ringing, Don said that it would be Kathy ringing after another crisis. We were both shattered so we just let it ring.

The next day I had the day off and the phone rang again.

It was the hospital.

They asked us if we knew Kathy. When we said we did, they told us that Kathy had been seriously injured in an 'incident' the night before. Sean had attacked her. This time, he had stabbed her in the neck with a knife and had very badly beaten her up.

She was in intensive care.

We raced up to the hospital to see her. She was in a terrible state. She eventually recovered but was very traumatised and her heroin addiction worsened as a result. Sean was charged with attacking her and not long after was also charged for armed robbery. As a result of both charges he was sent to prison.

With Sean was out of the way, Kathy continued working the clubs and taking heroin and seemed much happier.

Then she suddenly disappeared.

Some time later, I had a letter come out of the blue, it was from Kathy. She had returned to Dublin and now had a baby boy by Sean, but her deeply religious family wouldn't have a 'Gurrier' which is what they called a child born out of wedlock and would have nothing to do with her or the child.

Speaking of religion reminds me of a Methodist Minister who once came to Greens Court. Complete with dog collar, he sat down and ordered a coke. Maggie and I sat with him while he excited himself talking about kinky things, including rubber and leather.

He also hinted that he would like to have sex with two women at the same time. Cassandra, being a good Catholic girl, couldn't wait to bring the bill over. He could only pay some of it, so we took all of his church details as a deposit while he went to get the rest of the money from a cash-point.
We knew we could take him for every penny.

He wouldn't have had a prayer if his church had found out what he was up to in our congregation.

At one point, Maggie and I rented a flat above a club called The Phoenix. The flats were quite swish but at that time we didn't care about things like that. It was just convenient for work and also the nightlife. It was quite a cosy place.

Adam was our neighbour. He was a good looking Glaswegian with long black hair (which he often tied up into a ball with chopsticks pushed through the middle) and wore a kilt. He loved the ladies and with his broad Glasgow accent the ladies loved him.
He was really into the music scene and worked the bar and the doors of Erotica and with his humour and charm was a very good barman.

Always in the mood for a party, Adam liked his drugs, cocaine and weed. He had been in Soho a long time, long before I had arrived, dealing drugs in the clubs.

His accent and weird dress sense ensured he stood out. He intimidated a lot of punters into paying up quite quickly just by his appearance but, he was always polite.

On one particular night, I was with a couple of friends at his flat having a drink and smoking a bit of weed.

All of a sudden he jumped up and said:

'Let's play Russian Roulette!'

We all looked at each other wondering what on earth he meant. I asked if he was joking. Laughing, he reached under the table, brought out a gun, put it to his head and pulled the trigger.

We just sat there in stunned disbelief, not knowing what to do.

Adam suddenly burst out laughing;

'It's only a starting pistol!'

I felt sick. I couldn't believe his head was still on his shoulders.
We were all stoned, it took a while to realise he was only kidding.

Adam was a hard man who practiced martial arts. He wasn't a thug, but he would stand up for himself when he believed he was in the right. He was a genuine guy who had the wit of Billy Connolly, making us cry with laughter. But, God help anyone who crossed him. Like the time an Australian punter went into Erotica. When the barman, a close friend of his and a Glaswegian he knew from back home, took the bill to the Australian, he started shouting and pushing him and the girls around, knocking one girl right over a table. Adam lost it and the Australian learnt a quick lesson about hitting out at women. Adam would not tolerate men hitting women.

He liked his clubbing. He always used to drink Black Russian's, but he also got The Intrepid Fox to buy milk in so he could drink White Russians, the same as Black Russians but with milk added to the Tia Maria and vodka.

We used a restaurant called The Meatpackers in those days, ordering massive jugs of Long Island iced tea and big plates of ribs and steak and then we'd go clubbing, sometimes to a club Adam introduced me to called Heaven. There were huge platforms scattered everywhere which had men dancing on them. The men wore only thongs. It was a gay club. It was under the railway arches in the West End, we all loved it and we spent a lot of nights in there. We knew most of the doormen, so we didn't pay to go in. It was one of our favourite nights out. Coming from a small town I'd never seen anything like that place. Adam introduced me to a whole other club scene.

One night, Maggie and I were just chilling out in our flat when there was a knock at the door. It was Adam. He came bouncing through the door announcing he was throwing a party that night and he wanted us all to meet in our second home, The Intrepid Fox.
It was all a bit sudden but a party was a party and it seemed rude to refuse.
I went to the bar and I was told drinks were free. Adam had put money behind the bar. I wondered why, things didn't quite feel right. I looked round for him and there he was, dressed to kill in Doc Marten's, a kilt and the signature chopsticks through the ball of hair on top of his head.

As usual, there were lots of women around him. He saw us and walked over and gave me a hug. Then strangely, just out of the blue he said:

'You need to sort your life out Max and look after that Irishman of yours.'

He gave me a big hug and a kiss then wandered off to make sure the party was going well. It was all a bit strange.

After we had got home, at around midnight, we had a knock on the door. I answered. There were two policemen standing there. They asked if we knew Scottish Adam.

'Yes, of course we do,' I replied.

They asked if they could come in and asked us to both sit down.

'We are sorry to have to tell you this, but Adam has taken his own life.'

We sat there shell-shocked for a minute and then the tears came.

We realised that we had just been at his leaving party.

The police left. We just stayed in the flat, numbed.

He was one of our closest friends.

'How could he do this?'

'Why did he do it?'

At this point I noticed there was a letter addressed to me, just sticking out of the bottom of the door, that I hadn't noticed earlier.

I opened it. It was from Adam.


You can love me, you can feel me, but you can never understand me.

I love you always,

Adam.

Later on the next day, we discovered what Adam had actually done. He walked to the nearest tube station, took a whole sheet of acid tablets and jumped in front of a train.

On the day he died, he posted a large amount of money to his dad in Scotland with a note instructing that the money was for his friends.
It was an invitation to his funeral to anyone who knew him.
They were to have a free bar, buy a lot of cocaine and party.

He had planned everything. His dad got the letter the same morning the police arrived at his door to say his son had taken his own life

*Adam, I hope you have found a place to settle.*
*I hope that you're still wearing those docs, kilt and kicking ass.*
*You are sadly missed but will you will never be forgotten.*

*Rest in peace my friend.*

# When We Laugh At the Fields of Regret

My parents had taken over a pub, The Kestrel in Hatton, Staffordshire. They had kept their house in Uttoxeter but they lived at the pub full time. I would go home on the odd weekend and I would sometimes score heroin from local sources, people who I knew from Uttoxeter.

One day, they asked if Don and I would think about leaving London, live up in the Midlands and work for them. It didn't sound like a bad idea.
It would be decent money without the chance of being arrested every day.
I did love London and the nightlife but it sounded too good an opportunity to turn down. I was getting older and Soho was changing in a way I didn't much like. I was still taking heroin but my habit had diminished, I was really only taking it when the urge was overwhelming. I wasn't continually stoned and was managing to get my life back together. I knew if we left I would miss the lifestyle. I had grown used to it over the fourteen years I had been in London but I also knew it was time to move on.

We were still debating whether to leave or stay in Soho, when things started happening to make our decision a lot easier. The law was coming down heavily on the clubs and girls who worked them and it was getting very hard to make decent money. It seemed everything was coming to an end.

I finally kicked the 'skag' just before we made the move. I went through hell with the withdrawal symptoms. That is something I do remember very clearly.

Coming off heroin is like having a fever, you feel freezing cold and are shivering but sweating at the same time. Your nose runs constantly. My legs used to ache terribly. At times it would feel as though someone was ripping the veins out of them. I had to use whole bottles of Benylin cough linctus just to sleep.
Don was brilliant while I was coming off heroin, always encouraging me and rubbing my legs to make the pain go away.

I did sometimes lapse. Heroin addicts are very similar to alcoholics; they will hide their drug anywhere. I was very crafty and I would hide supplies of heroin in the bathroom. I would say I was going for a long soak and then take it without Don knowing. I would also take speed so Don would not spot that my eyes were pinned. The lapses carried on for around 4 years before I finally kicked the drug.

We moved up to the Midlands. At first, we found it hard to adjust to the far slower lifestyle but after a while began to enjoy the laid back way of life that everyone seemed to have.

Once there I never touched heroin again.

Don and I had the whole of the upstairs of the pub, which was a three bedroom flat. There was a bungalow built onto the side of the pub, which my parents lived in. As I had done a catering course in the past I helped the chef with the cooking. I also did cellar work, acted as a bar-person and waited on the tables in the restaurant. Don's official title was cellar-man but he also helped out where needed. We settled in quite nicely.

It worked quite well; Don and I always got on well and worked well together. We stayed at the pub for about ten years.

Some of the staff would go to a pub in Tutbury, called The Castle, we'd play pool there and socialise after a hard days work. The Castle is a whole story of its own. Nicknamed 'Beirut' by the locals, the barman looked like something from the Beverley Hillbillies. He was bald with a long beard and worked behind the bar wearing a vest, which frankly, had seen better days.

They had two or three Alsatian dogs and there would be dog shit all over the place, you would have to watch where you put your feet as you went to the bar for a drink.

It wouldn't be anybody's first choice for a cosy drink at the local, but it was the only pub in the area which did a late bar and we could go there after work.

I also used to go up to the New Inn to watch the football on a Sunday sometimes and would say to my father,

'Ey up dad would you like a paper from the shop?'

It was a running joke because my father knew he would not see the newspaper till around midnight or the next day at best.

But he would always say in his broad Nottinghamshire lilt,

'Yeah alright duck, I'll see you later!'

He was a lovely man my dad.

I used to have a mate called Kaz who came with me to the New Inn. We were sat in the lounge one day and I noticed someone mouthing off about football in the bar.

Kaz told me she knew him, and that he had no interest in women he was just mad about football. I bet her a tenner that I could pull him. I sent Kaz's sister, who was a barmaid at the time, to tell the man to come in and talk to us. The man, whose name was Steve said,

'Bollocks, if she wants to talk to me she can come round here.'

I certainly wasn't going to go into the bar for him so that attempt fizzled out, but the bet was still on.

The following week, I made my usual trip up to the New Inn on the Sunday and Steve was in the lounge playing darts. Kaz was a good darts player and had played for the county so we played with him. I got talking to Steve and we got on well, like a house on fire. After that, I saw him regularly in the pub every Sunday for darts.

Steve became a regular at The Kestrel.

My mum and I had an argument one day over a member of staff who I insisted we should sack. My mum didn't agree and I gave her an ultimatum, they would go or I would. The member of staff wasn't sacked so Don and I left the pub and moved to Nottingham. Don got a job and I fell pregnant. Losing the baby this time was not an option. I was no longer on heroin and we were both settled in the Midlands, so Don had no reason to object. We moved into a house in St Anne's. Steve, who had become a friend of Don's, had some problems with the place he had been living at and moved in with us temporarily.

I had a beautiful baby girl and life seemed to be panning out well for us, but Steve living with us didn't work out and after a couple of months he left.

After a while it became apparent Don and I had grown apart. I now had a daughter and was ready for the family life. Don still wanted to go out partying and live a rock n' roll lifestyle. Don and I decided we would go our separate ways and I moved to Burton with my daughter.

Steve was living in Burton at the time; on reflection I am wondering did I follow him there? Steve didn't want anything to do with me; he had got back in with his sister, who hated me with a passion and had put him off the idea of getting together with me.

One day Steve and I bumped into each other. We started seeing each other and he would be always popping over to have his tea with me, even though we lived in separate flats. Again, we got on like a house on fire and after a short while Steve asked me if we would like to move in with him.

We moved in together in Burton and eventually moved to Uttoxeter.

I have been with Steve for 8 years and I am very settled.

There will always be a part of my heart left in the West End, as they were very happy days. Sometimes when I sit at home on my own, if Steve and the kids are out, I reminisce about my days in Soho. I get all my old photographs out and I think to myself 'what am I doing here, in a quiet family environment?' and hark back to the old West End days.
They were exciting and eventful times and possibly I look back at them with rose tinted glasses. I am sure if I was put back there today in today's climate of escalating drug and gun crime, reality would be a totally different thing.

I did keep in contact with a couple of people from Soho. Greens Court ended up becoming a crack-den more than it was a club and eventually was closed down.

Most of the girls were doing crack as I left for my new life.

Not long after I had gone, three punters went into Greens Court and sat with a hostess. When the bill was presented they began shouting and pushing their way out of the club. It all got quite intense and eventually the three punters left without paying. Things went quiet for a while but when the buzzer went again, it was the same three lads. This time they were armed with a gun.
They shot Cassandra.

She was taken off in an ambulance and thankfully survived, but that was the end of Greens Court.

It wasn't the first time in the Soho clubs that something so serious had happened, and I am sure it won't be the last which is very sad.
The people who work in such places are just people trying to make a living.

Recently I went been back to visit Soho.
Accompanied by my co-author we toured the streets. The sex industry is now a shadow of its former self. There are only about three clubs left and Soho seemed to have lost the buzz I remember it having.

Walking through the little alleyways still excited me however, and memories flooded back, some happy and some sad.

One thing for definite, I will never forget the times I had and the friendships I forged along the way.

I hope I haven't shocked too many people with this insight into being a hostess in Soho, as I loved the lifestyle.

If I had the chance to go back and do it all again I probably would.......

*In a report published in February 2009, a senior police officer claimed that fake prostitutes (clippers) and drug dealers are still plentiful and operating in Soho. Detective Chief Supt Andy Rowell claims that fake prostitutes and drug dealers outnumber genuine ones on the streets of Soho in London's West End.*

*Soho prostitutes have always, and still do work inside Soho flats and premises, but those on the street are mostly, all fake.*

*There have been many clean up campaigns in this notorious area up by police and it is now mainly con-artists targeting gullible foreign tourists and out-of-town visitors.*

*There could be as much as double the amount of fake drug dealers as real ones that con the unsuspecting into buying boot polish or liquorice as cannabis, wax wrapped in foil as crack cocaine and aspirin pills, with the markings rubbed off as various tablets.*

*A hardcore of about 15 fake prostitutes work by taking a "deposit for a room" and then disappearing, or enticing a punter into an alleyway where a male accomplice steals their money. The victims are usually too embarrassed to report the crimes.*

*It is estimated that a lot of the women 'clippers' are the remnants of Soho clip-joints which have closed down in recent years. There could be as many as twenty 20 fake drug dealers targeting the area, mostly at weekends in the early hours.*

*The fake street prostitutes and drug dealers are from various criminal gangs that travel to Soho from other parts of London like Lambeth, Southwark and Camden. The detective in charge of the area, said: 'A lot of visitors are thinking in the past, these days Soho has been cleaned-up.*

*Yet hundreds of visitors from out of London come to Soho after the theatres have emptied looking for illegal after-hours activities. Their image of Soho is sadly out-of-date. We are continuing to step up our efforts at clamping down on these types of crime and we've largely succeeded. Soho is now a safe place to come and enjoy yourself, but please don't come looking for drugs and prostitutes. You will almost certainly get something you didn't expect.'*

# ALSO BY VHC PUBLISHING

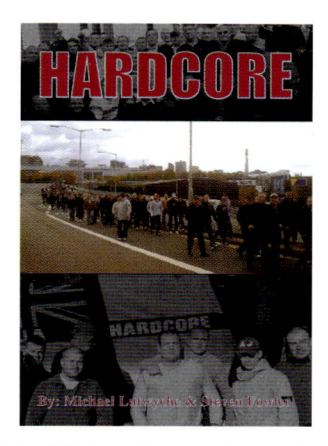

**'Hardcore' by Michael Lutwyche & Steven Fowler.**

*'a lot more intense than other books on the subject, with regular stories of savage woundings taken and given out.......That I began to get an insight into such mentality is a tribute to the writers. They certainly leave a lasting impression......'*

The true story of Steven Fowler and Aston Villa Hardcore - one of English footballs most prolific hooligan gangs.
Villa Hardcore were one of the most active English football 'firms' of the 90s & 00's. Fowler has been branded a 'Hooligan general feared the world over' Birmingham Post April 2nd 2002. His Villa Hardcore were labelled 'one of the two worst firms on the England international front' Daily Mirror January 12th 1998. Villa Hardcore were investigated by the security forces as well as the police. Fowler and fellow members of the gang were thrown out of France in 1998. He was subsequently refused entry into Belgium and Holland for Euro 2000 and arrested in Japan in 2002 for attempting to enter the country. Sentences totalling over 100 years were handed out to participants in a series of high profile incidents involving Villa Hardcore. They have been branded as 'scum' and 'a disgrace to their city' by a judge. There are currently over 80 Villa Hardcore members serving football banning orders. In this 'warts and all' book they give their side of the story.

Available at WH Smiths, HMV and Borders.
Also online at www.vhcpublishing.com